ENDORSEMENTS

The Road Home by Sarah and Isabell Bowling is a powerful, hope-filled guide to help all of us identify the "prodigal within" and to find the Father we all long for. With profound insight, they offer practical wisdom and encouragement rooted in Scripture. This book is formatted with invitation for interaction and activation, which makes it a perfect tool for personal reflection, group Bible study, and family devotions. Sarah and Isabell's compassionate and grace-filled approach not only brings comfort but stirs hope and faith for breakthrough and new beginnings. If you are believing for personal breakthrough or for the return of a prodigal who is close to your heart, *The Road Home* is an essential tool that will empower you with hope. I highly recommend this valuable, anointed resource!

Patricia King
Founder of Patricia King Ministries

Understanding the Father heart of God is key to recognizing our position as His children. Without that, we cannot really be anchored in His promises. Sarah and Isabell have taken one of the most familiar stories in the Bible, "The Prodigal Son," and delved into the heart of our Father, both for those who *stray* and those who *stay*. His love is steadfast and available. It never ceases or comes to an end. It is new every morning! Great is His faithfulness! What a Father!

Terry Meeuwsen
Co-host, *The 700 Club*
Founder, Orphan's Promise

T0361716

Sarah and Isabell have done it again with *The Road Home*. For many, home is our safe haven, but for others it's a place of pain and shame. Sarah and Isabell use the parable of the Prodigal Son to call us home to the heart of the Father who absorbs our past and renews our future. *The Road Home* draws you into the story by telling stories of real people and their own home trauma and triumph. Before you know it, their stories elicit your own, so you find yourself running home to the heart of the Father and His inexplicably good embrace.

Mark Moore

My good friend, Sarah Bowling, and her daughter, Isabell, have outdone themselves with their book, *The Road Home*, which they co-authored. This is a great read for anyone who has lost their way in life and is looking for the hope of some semblance of a return to the good life they had once experienced. It will also be helpful to parents and family members of those children and siblings who have allowed wrong choices to separate them from their family whose hearts are broken for them. I really enjoyed the modern allegory of the story of the Prodigal Son written by Isabell Bowling. I believe God will touch your heart, as it did mine, as you find yourself in the story of this book, *The Road Home*.

Greg Mohr
Founder of Greg Mohr Ministries
Director of Ministry School and
Staff Instructor at Charis Bible College

THE

ROAD

HOME

THE
ROAD
HOME

THE FATHER'S INVITATION

SARAH BOWLING
ISABELL BOWLING

DESTINY IMAGE® PUBLISHERS, INC.
P.O. Box 310, Shippensburg, PA 17257-0310
"Publishing cutting-edge prophetic resources to supernaturally empower the body of Christ"

This book and all other Destiny Image and Destiny Image Fiction books are available at Christian bookstores and distributors worldwide.

For more information on foreign distributors, call 717-532-3040.
Reach us on the Internet: www.destinyimage.com.

ISBN 13 TP: 979-8-8815-0242-3
ISBN 13 eBook: 979-8-8815-0243-0

For Worldwide Distribution, Printed in the U.S.A.
1 2 3 4 5 6 7 8 / 29 28 27 26 25

DEDICATION

I'm dedicating this book to Cathy. Thank you very much for helping me experience home—your friendship and generosity are nothing less than holy and divine!

Sarah Bowling

For Pastors AJ and AdriElle.
Every prodigal needs friends like you.

Isabell Bowling

CONTENTS

INTRODUCTION

Of everything I've ever written, perhaps this project is the most intimidating to me. I'm intimidated by it because I think it's possibly the most concise yet powerful telling of God our Father engaging humanity, regardless of who we are, what we've done, or what we haven't done, regardless of our choices, failures, achievements, perfections, and flaws.

I've read this parable almost every day for close to a year, and even though I've read it hundreds of times, I still find myself continually undone by its message.

I pray that as you read this book, you will experience God's presence, which is authentic love. I pray that our Heavenly Father guides you to your home with Him, reconciling whatever might be keeping you from being family with Him.

PART ONE

THE YOUNGER SON

Jesus continued: "There was a man who had two sons. The younger one said to his father, 'Father, give me my share of the estate.' So he divided his property between them.

"Not long after that, the younger son got together all he had, set off for a distant country and there squandered his wealth in wild living. After he had spent everything, there was a severe famine in that whole country, and he began to be in need. So he went and hired himself out to a citizen of that country, who sent him to his fields to feed pigs. He longed to fill his stomach with the pods that the pigs were eating, but no one gave him anything.

"When he came to his senses, he said, 'How many of my father's hired men have food to spare, and here I am starving to death! I will set out and go back to my father and say to him: Father, I have sinned against heaven and against you. I am no longer worthy to be called your son; make me like one of your hired men.' So he got up and went to his father.

"But while he was still a long way off, his father saw him and was filled with compassion for him; he ran to his son, threw his arms around him and kissed him.

"The son said to him, 'Father, I have sinned against heaven and against you. I am no longer worthy to be called your son.'

"But the father said to his servants, 'Quick! Bring the best robe and put it on him. Put a ring on his finger and sandals on his feet. Bring the fattened calf and kill it. Let's have a feast and celebrate. For this son of mine was dead and is alive again; he was lost and is found.' So they began to celebrate.

"Meanwhile, the older son was in the field. When he came near the house, he heard music and dancing. So he called one of the servants and asked him what was going on. 'Your brother has come,' he replied, 'and your father has killed the fattened calf because he has him back safe and sound.'

"The older brother became angry and refused to go in. So his father went out and pleaded with him. But he answered his father, 'Look! All these years I've been slaving for you and never disobeyed your orders. Yet you never gave me even a young goat so I could celebrate with my friends. But when this son of yours who has squandered your property with prostitutes comes home, you kill the fattened calf for him!'

"'My son,' the father said, 'you are always with me, and everything I have is yours. But we had to celebrate and be glad, because this brother of yours was dead and is alive again; he was lost and is found'" (Luke 15:11-32 NIV).

CHAPTER ONE

GETTING HOME

"I wish I could live here!" This is what I thought sometime in my mid-teens when I was having dinner at my friend's house. Her dad had just teased me about pretty much anything, and her mom had made tuna surprise, the family's least favorite dinner. When everyone groaned as their mom set the casserole dish on the table, she quickly announced, "I also made fresh chocolate chip cookies for dessert, and we have some vanilla ice cream to go with the cookies!" Everyone seemed to accept the chocolate chip cookie goal to survive the tuna surprise casserole.

I like being at my friend's home for lots of reasons, including Rose, her big German Shepherd, getting to complain about food I didn't like (which wasn't allowed at my house), candy that was easily stolen from the candy dish in the formal parlor, and her mom's quirky humor. My friend's home was different from my home in all the right ways.

When I was sixteen, I got my driver's license. I suddenly had the ability to visit my friends, drive myself to basketball games, visit the library, and drive to the mall to eat delicious ice cream and play my favorite video games. I got my license in the dark ages when we didn't have cell phones. Because of that, we used paper maps—the fold up kind that was sold at gas stations. I quickly learned the value of such maps because I didn't enjoy getting lost. I wanted to make sure that I always knew how to get home, no matter where I drove.

When you think about "home," you might remember some place you lived when you were young. Maybe you lived in the same house all throughout your youth. Or maybe you lived in a few different places for various reasons. It is also possible that you spent your childhood in a nomadic existence, moving as the stable constant rather than a single location being the constant. What home was like throughout your upbringing has a significant effect on what home means for you as an adult.

With this thinking, let's consider Jesus' parable about the Prodigal Son. It is an interesting journey into some key influences, like home and family. It's also noteworthy to look at the immediate context for this parable because the context can help us to appreciate and possibly identify with the audiences who heard Jesus tell this parable. If we only read the Prodigal Son without considering to whom Jesus was telling this parable and what its context was, we'll miss some important applications for our lives. It is an unhelpful practice only to read what Jesus said and did without making any personal connections or applications.

Audience

When we look at the beginning of Luke 15, where the Prodigal Son parable is found, we see that Jesus is talking to two groups of people. In Luke 15:1-3 (NASB) we read, "Now all the tax collectors and the sinners were coming near Him to listen to Him. Both the Pharisees and the scribes began to grumble, saying, 'This man receives sinners and eats with them.' So

He told them this parable." From this launching point, Jesus tells three parables about things that are lost: a lost sheep, a lost coin, and a lost son. But before we delve into the lost or Prodigal Son story, let's consider to whom Jesus is telling these parables.

In the first verse of Luke 15, we read that tax collectors and sinners were coming to listen to Jesus. At this time in history and in the nation of Israel, tax collectors were scum of the earth people. The tax collectors were folk who used brawn, muscle, coercion, intimidation, and bullying to extract money from the Jews to give to the Roman oppressors living in Israel at that time. Additionally, sinners were the non-religious people who didn't conform to righteous and upstanding living. Both of these groups were coming to listen to Jesus. It is interesting to note that "unrighteous and unholy" people wanted to hear what Jesus had to say, specifically making an effort to gather and listen to Him. Maybe these kinds of people were attracted to Jesus, since He was known to be a friend to sinners (Matthew 11:19).

"Unrighteous and unholy" people wanted to hear what Jesus had to say.

In contrast to the curious sinners and tax collectors, the scribes and Pharisees (religious people), were cranky and grumbly. They took issue with Jesus' welcoming posture toward the people who weren't pious and who didn't aim for religious purity or rigor. On more than one occasion in the Gospels, we see lots of tensions and conflicts between Jesus and the religious leaders and influencers around Him. It is no surprise that these folks were gripey with Jesus. There was plenty of disdain and disgust from these religious folk aimed at everyone who was less than pious or righteous.

It's important for us to keep these two groups of people in mind when we read the Prodigal Son parable because of the reflections and associations found in each son. The younger son could be likened to the sinners and tax collectors, while the older son could be described as dutiful and upstanding. We should think about which character we might be in the parable (older son, younger son, father) as well as which kind of audience member who was listening to Jesus we might be (tax collector, sinner, religious devotee, etc.). Over the course of this book, I'll come back to these audiences to remind us of their respective characters in this story.

I also want to point out that in this parable, none of the main characters (the younger son, older son, or father) acted according to expected social, religious, familial, or conventional norms. The younger son wasn't supposed to ask his dad for his inheritance before his dad died. The older son was supposed to be his father's "right hand man." And the father in this parable wasn't supposed to "chase" his sons, give out an inheritance prematurely, or humble himself by doing all the relationship work with extravagant generosity.

For now, it's important to think about how each character didn't act according to customary expectations. I suspect that in unique ways, some of your upbringing, family members, or experiences didn't go according to cultural norms of "healthy" family interactions and environments. I have a friend who always laughs when she says, "My family put the 'fun' in dysfunctional!" So maybe you didn't grow up in a *Leave It to Beaver* home. Maybe your home looked more like *The Brady Bunch, Young Sheldon, The Fosters, The Addams Family, The Simpsons, South Park,* or others.

In helping us to think about this parable and its application to our lives today, I'm including a brief description of the families of many of my friends and acquaintances in most chapters. These are called, "Family Insights," and I think you'll find them helpful as you also consider your upbringing and homelife. I've obscured facts, locations, and details of these stories as I'm intent on protecting the identities of everyone I interviewed. Some of the families you'll read about were amazing, some were neutral, and some were sheer hell. No matter where they lay on the spectrum, all families are a variety of blessings and curses. Here's your first introduction to one of my friends.

Family Insight

My name is John, and I grew up in a really small town in the Midwest. My town was so small that our high school was the central school for several towns like mine, and my graduating class had twenty-four people in it.

I grew up with four siblings, and all of us had different dads, which makes us all half brothers and sisters. My home was always clean and well taken care of, even though my parents each worked at least two to three jobs every week. They both worked very hard and did their best to provide a comfortable home and steady meals.

My mom was an incredible woman, and I don't think there's anything she couldn't do. She sewed all of our clothes, including our jeans. She cooked delicious family meals, packed our school lunches every day, and worked several jobs to help with household expenses. My mom was always present for me, no matter what. I have always been wholly secure in my mom's love for me.

My dad was also present for me, going to my athletic competitions and events, teaching me to hunt, fish, and play various sports, and teaching me car maintenance. He was a very hard worker, like my mom, even though he was a functional alcoholic. When he drank, which was a few nights a week, he was lots nicer than when he was sober. When he was sober, he was a harsh disciplinarian, probably because his own upbringing was horrific.

Even with the tasty food that mom made, our family dinners were never enjoyable when my dad was home. He had the view that children should be seen and not heard, and he firmly enforced etiquette rules, quiet order, and appropriate silverware usage. For me, dinner when my dad was home was extremely tense and very unpleasant.

Nevertheless, I'm extremely grateful for my upbringing. I'm glad I had parents who were attentive and consistently present. I learned integrity and manhood from my dad, and I learned compassion and nurture from my mom. As for my siblings, I'm most close with my sister, although all of us keep in touch fairly often and have great respect for who we are as adults.

As we come to the end of this chapter, you'll find an R&R (Reflect and Respond) section for you to work through as you begin to process and engage with the content in this book and Jesus' parable. These R&R sections are found at the end of each chapter and are important exercises to help you get the most out of this book. They will help you see ways that your Heavenly Father can redeem your upbringing and root you firmly in your place as His son or daughter.

You'll also note throughout the upcoming chapters that there are repeated sections pertaining to the "Culture and History" when Jesus told this parable, along with the repetition of "Celebration and Party" that happens with each of the main characters. Furthermore, you'll also read about "The Help" who are secondary characters in the thinking and interactions for each of these main characters. These individuals are the servants and household help that serve as a support role in various ways to each member of the family in this parable. Finally, you'll note that there are some "Family Values" peppered throughout this book, and these will be helpful observation points to see the values of our Heavenly Father working in the context of His children and our relationship with our Father.

If there's one takeaway I'd pray for you as you read the following chapters, it would be that 1 John 3:1 would become your daily reality. I suspect that if we truly live in this reality, we will exude life, love, redemption, and reconciliation!

See how great a love the Father has bestowed on us, that we would be called children of God; and such we are (1 John 3:1 NASB).

If we truly live in this reality, we will exude life, love, redemption, and reconciliation!

In the following sections of this book, we'll take an in-depth look at each of the sons as well as the father in the parable to unpack who they are and to consider some ways that we could be each person in the parable. Let's begin *The Road Home!*

CHAPTER ONE:
GETTING HOME

R&R: Reflect and Respond

1. Describe your upbringing, starting with your parents. Did one or both of them work? What kinds of things did your parents struggle with: anxiety, depression, addiction, OCD, workaholic, codependency, psychosis, shame, etc.?

_____

_____

2. Do you have siblings? How many brothers / sisters? Where do you fit in the lineup of your siblings? Briefly describe each sibling.

_____

_____

3. What was an average school day like for you in elementary school? Who was your favorite teacher? Why? Least favorite teacher? Why?

_____

_____

4. How would you describe yourself in high school? Were you studious? Did you mostly goof off? Did you attend most of your classes or did you cut a lot of classes? Were grades important to you? Did you play any sports? Participate in any clubs? Join any organizations? Who were your friends in high school?

_____

_____

5. How did your relationship with your parents change when you entered elementary school? In high school? As an adult?

_____

_____

6. In what ways has your relationship with God been impacted by your upbringing?

_____

_____

7. How was your upbringing different than you think it should have been?

_____

_____

8. How did your parents express their love to you? Describe an experience with your parents when you felt very loved.

_____

_____

PART ONE

THE YOUNGER SON

Now all the tax collectors and the sinners were coming near Him to listen to Him. Both the Pharisees and the scribes began to grumble, saying, "This man receives sinners and eats with them" (Luke 15:1-2 NASB).

And He said, "A man had two sons. The younger of them said to his father, 'Father, give me the share of the estate that falls to me.' So he divided his wealth between them. And not many days later, the younger son gathered everything together and went on a journey into a distant country, and there he squandered his estate with loose living. Now when he had spent everything, a severe famine occurred in that country, and he began to be impoverished. So he went and hired himself out to one of the citizens of that country, and he sent him into his fields to feed swine. And he would have gladly filled his stomach with the pods that the swine were eating, and no one was giving anything to him. But when he came to his senses, he said, 'How many of my father's hired men have more than enough bread, but I am dying here with hunger! I will get up and go to my father, and will say to him, "Father, I have sinned against heaven, and in your sight; I am no longer worthy to be called your son; make me as one of your hired men."' So he got up and came to his father. But while he was still a long way off, his father saw him and felt compassion for him, and ran and embraced him and kissed him. And the son said to him, 'Father, I have sinned against heaven and in your sight; I am no longer worthy to be called your son.' But the father said to his slaves, 'Quickly bring out the best robe and put it on him, and put a ring on his hand and sandals on his feet; and bring the fattened calf, kill it, and let us eat and celebrate; for this son of mine was dead and has come to life again; he was lost and has been found.' And they began to celebrate.

Now his older son was in the field, and when he came and approached the house, he heard music and dancing. And he summoned one of the servants and began inquiring what these things could be. And he said to him, 'Your brother has come, and your father has killed the fattened calf because he has received him back safe and sound.' But he became angry and was not willing to go in; and his father came out and began pleading with him. But he answered and said to his father, 'Look! For so many years I have been serving you and I have never neglected a command of yours; and yet you have never given me a young goat, so that I might celebrate with my friends; but when this son of yours came, who has devoured your wealth with prostitutes, you killed the fattened calf for him.' And he said to him, 'Son, you have always been with me, and all that is mine is yours. But we had to celebrate and rejoice, for this brother of yours was dead and has begun to live, and was lost and has been found'" (Luke 15:11-32 NASB).

CHAPTER TWO

PARTY, PLEASURE, AND DEBAUCHERY

The younger of them said to his father, "Father, give me the share of the estate that falls to me." So he divided his wealth between them. And not many days later, the younger son gathered everything together and went on a journey into a distant country, and there he squandered his estate with loose living

(Luke 15:12-13 NASB).

"Let's PARTY!" I imagine this was the mantra for the younger son when he left his home after having acquired his share of the inheritance from his dad. Have you had a time or season in your life when "party" was your mantra and endgame? The concept of party can have a vast array of meanings, including everything from a small birthday party for a kindergartener to a drunken and drug-overflowing frat party that hopefully has some safeguards in place. Parties can be wonderful celebrations for milestones, and oftentimes, the party mindset can begin when we set aside being dutiful and responsible to have fun.

Thinking about being less responsible and having fun, I'm reminded of my first semester of college. I had a blast! This was my first time to live away from home and experience more autonomy and independence. I attended Oral Roberts University, which is a conservative Christian university in Tulsa, Oklahoma, and I lived in the dorms. Students who attended ORU signed an honor code (no drinking, sex, cheating, etc.), so the typical college party scene looked very different for me. While I didn't do any drinking, drugs, sex, etc., I definitely enjoyed my first semester of freedom! I was irresponsible and enjoyed the freedoms to make my own choices. Those choices included dating, staying up all night with new friends, goofing off with lots of practical jokes, and doing stupid stuff. My grades reflected my irresponsibility. So, the next semester, I buckled down and figured out a better balance between fun and grades.

When I enjoyed my party semester at university, it was a little bit like the younger son in the prodigal story moving to a foreign land to party; however, there are some differences that we should consider to gain a deeper understanding of what Jesus is saying in this parable. If we look at the history and culture of the time in which Jesus told this story, we will see some hotspots and stress points.

Culture and History

For starters, inheritance distribution for a typical Jewish family happened after the death of the father. Consequently, when the younger son asked the father for his share of the estate, his request was the same as telling his dad that he wanted him dead so that he could get his inheritance. Obviously, this would have been a very hurtful and dishonoring request.

*When the younger son asked the father for his share
of the estate, his request was the same as telling his
dad that he wanted him dead so that he could get his
inheritance.*

This would be offensive even in our day and culture, but
back in Jesus' day and in the Jewish culture, the demand of the
younger son was totally horrific! If a son made this request, the
father could choose to ostracize the son and consider him dead
to the family. Everyone in the community would understand.
Not only would the family ostracize a son for such a horrific
request, but all the household servants would shun such a disrespectful son.

On top of all the rejection this son would experience at home,
his village would also vilify the son. Indeed, there was a practice
called *kezazah* during which a son who had lost his family's
money among gentiles would be cut off from his village.[1] The
son's request would be equivalent to severing his relationship
and connection with his dad, home, family, community, village,
tribe, and country.

After receiving his part of the inheritance from his dad,
this son left his father, family, and home—everything that had
been his stability. He traveled to a distant country where he
partied away his inheritance. Consider how a few different
Bible translations describe the actions of the younger son in
Luke 15:13.

*It wasn't long before the younger son packed his bags
and left for a distant country. There, undisciplined and
dissipated, he wasted everything he had* (MSG).

A few days later this younger son packed all his belongings and moved to a distant land, and there he wasted all his money in wild living (NLT).

Not many days later, the younger son gathered all he had and took a journey into a far country, and there he squandered his property in reckless living (ESV).

Not long after that, the younger son got together all he had, set off for a distant country and there squandered his wealth in wild living (NIV).

Shortly afterward, the younger son packed up all his belongings and traveled off to see the world. He journeyed to a far-off land where he soon wasted all he was given in a binge of extravagant and reckless living (TPT).

It's interesting to consider the verbs that are used to describe what he did with his inheritance in the foreign country: wasted, squandered, dispersed, scattered. The Greek word that is used here has the idea of throwing chaff to the wind, or even the idea of winnowing. But instead of chaff, the youngest son is throwing away or squandering his inheritance, never to be recovered.

In the upcoming section for the father in the prodigal parable, we'll discuss in greater detail the importance and the historical and cultural contexts of inheritance, but in the meantime, the younger son is in a foreign country wasting away his inheritance. What could it look like, at this time in history, to party hard? Of course, they didn't have the sophisticated and manufactured drugs that are used today such as LSD, ecstasy, ketamine, etc. Nevertheless, in Jesus' era, partying had the same concepts and goals that we see with modern partying: have fun, relax, lower one's inhibitions, exhale, do what feels good, and maximize pleasure. I'd suggest that the decision the younger son made to go to a distant country would give him even greater opportunities to party since it would be unlikely that word would get back to his family or home village about his riotous living.

Family Insight

My name is Michelle, and I'm from a small town in Idaho. My upbringing was utter chaos. I attribute this pandemonium to the fact that my mom grew up in a family of alcoholics and her mom (my grandmother) died when she was about two or three years old. The siblings of my mom's husband were all put in psychiatric wards; however, he wasn't loads more sane than his brothers and sisters.

I don't refer to my mom's husband as my dad, because he wasn't my biological father, even though he was the father for my older sister. I'm not quite sure who my biological father was, as there was lots of static and continual tension around that subject in my home. As for my sister, her father doted on her, which was an obvious contrast to his disregard for me.

Because we lived in such a small town, I was free to roam, explore, adventure, experiment, and meander pretty much anywhere and anytime. I did lots of "meandering," showing up for dinner at various people's houses. I knew they would look with kindness on me, even though I was basically a feral child.

I also had good reason to be feral because my house was "unpleasant." There were often fights that included vases flying through the air and smashing into a million pieces against a wall, inconsistent meals, clutter, moldy food, unkempt and dirty clothing, missing shoes, etc. Layer all of this with a mom who struggled to be kind, supportive, attentive, and compassionate and it gets really obvious why I chose to be wild rather than "domesticated" in such a BS house.

Our house was in continual conflict mode. As an example, I remember my mom's husband getting so angry with my mom that he took all her clothes in the middle of winter, threw them in a snowbank, and poured hot water on them so that they froze, and my mom had nothing to wear. In turn, she yelled at him, bleached his clothes, and hid the keys to his car. I don't know what happened after that, because I ran across the street, barefoot, to find some calm and sanity at the neighbor's house.

My mom was an alcoholic, so I learned to rely on myself, to protect myself, and to survive by persistence, hard work, and being people smart. These skills have served me well. At the same time, I'm keenly aware that I'm the adult child of an alcoholic, so there is lots of baggage that goes with that!

Celebration and Party

As mentioned in the last chapter, over the course of this parable, we will see that each of the main characters (younger son, older son, and father) all have different experiences with parties and celebrations. Each of them has a different goal or purpose for a party, along with different people who enjoy and celebrate at the respective parties. For the younger son, his party experiences were with random foreigners to enjoy himself and live with frivolity.

Let's keep in mind that celebrations were big events at this time in history. Each of the main characters discusses and values celebrations. This younger son moved away from his family and village to celebrate and party. He chose to party away far away from everyone and everything he knew, disconnected from any core, grounding, familiar community, or familial relationships. What had been earned by his dad, along with the accumulation of wealth by his family for generations, was frittered away.

With his inheritance, he bought momentary pleasure, frivolous purchases, disloyal acquaintances, and temporary fun. However he spent his inheritance in this distant country, he burned through all of it with nothing to show from his party choices. No friends remained, the food and drink were consumed, purchased clothes had no value, and all his fun evaporated into froth. There was nothing left to show from his wasteful living. Riotous, reckless, wild, and unrestrained choices left this son destitute.

There was nothing left to show from his wasteful living.

Maybe he woke up in a hangover haze late one morning and reached for his money belt to continue his party living but was not able to find it. Maybe he stumbled around, looking for his clothes, dizzy from the previous night's drunken soiree. I suspect that he looked around for his party friends and was perplexed to see that no one was around. What if his fair-weather friends had taken the rest of the money from his inheritance, stole his best clothes, and left him with only a few scraps of rotted, maggoty meat, some stale bread, and half a glass of the cheap booze?

Family Insights

My name is Andrea, and I'm the oldest daughter of six kids. The oldest among the six kids is my brother who is still the "pillar" in our family to this day. Unfortunately, my parents both died in my teen years. My dad was killed by a drunk driver when I was fifteen, and my mom died a slow and gory death from brain cancer, finally succumbing to that horrific disease when I was eighteen.

Because she was diagnosed with the cancer when I was twelve, all of us kids had to step up and be more mature than the friends who were our ages. At the same time, my dad was lots more attentive to my older brother and made sure that he got to play little league baseball, went to Boy Scouts, played rec league soccer, and had good clothes and shoes. The rest of us either got his hand-me-downs or did thrift store shopping with my mom, prioritizing the best deals over fashion.

Both of my parents worked full-time jobs to feed, clothe, and provide a home for all of us. I grew up understanding that "money doesn't grow on trees." This meant that I worked lots of jobs like babysitting, mowing lawns, selling lemonade, clipping coupons from the Saturday newspaper, and securing any odd jobs that could give me a few dollars. My older brother, however, didn't have to do any of this because my dad made sure that he had whatever he needed and wanted.

During family dinners, my mom catered to my dad and brother, bringing their meals to them to eat from their TV trays as they watched whatever sport was playing in that season. The rest of us took our plates to eat in our rooms or somewhere around the house, since the kitchen was too small to accommodate the rest of the family. Additionally, our house was continually messy—I was often embarrassed when my friends would come over. I could see their distaste for the chaotic condition of our house.

When my mom was diagnosed with brain cancer, this was a defining moment in my upbringing because her health declined over the next six years. When she had various surgeries and treatments, my aunt (her sister), came to town occasionally to help at the house, but mostly we were left to look after ourselves. Despite her terminal illness, I knew that my mom loved me, and I knew that she was abundantly sad that she wasn't able to be a "regular mom."

We all went to public school, as there wasn't money for anything beyond that, including any sports, clubs, music lessons, etc. We also always signed up for the school lunch program, given our financial struggles. Riding the bus to school let my parents leave for their jobs early in the day, and when we came home from school, we watched TV and sometimes did some household chores. Needless to say, we didn't do extracurricular activities in school, unless we could work out our own rides and pay our way from whatever money we could earn.

If I had to pick just a few adjectives to describe my childhood, I'd say that it was chaotic and stony.

In returning to our parable, it's possible that the scenario of waking up with a hangover, no money, rotted food, and MIA friends could describe what happened to this son when all of his inheritance, along with everything and everyone he had bought, was gone. Luke 15:14 begins with, "Now when he had *spent everything*." In Greek, the word for "spent everything" is δαπανάω.[2] This word is used five times in the New Testament, and it always has the idea of spending everything to the point of utter depletion. It means having nothing left, nothing to show for what you spent your resources on, resulting in a state of being wholly empty and lacking.

Sobering up and realizing his impoverished condition was probably a rude and horrific awakening. Indeed, it's a brutal epiphany when you must face the results of poor and irresponsible choices, particularly when you have no resources available to attempt to reverse such foolish decisions. This is the condition of the younger son when he had burned through all of his inheritance. Choices and consequences are often inseparable twins. Things go from bad to awful for this son, as we'll see in the next chapter.

CHAPTER TWO:
PARTY, PLEASURE, AND DEBAUCHERY

R&R: Reflect and Respond

1. Describe a season in your life when you made choices to prioritize pleasures over responsibilities.

_____

_____

2. How did this season make you feel? How did this season affect your life?

_____

_____

3. What were some positive outcomes for you from this season? Negative outcomes?

_____

_____

4. How did your choices in this season affect your family?

_____

_____

5. Has anyone in your family squandered wealth (money, time, energy)? What did you think and how did you feel when you watched this happen?

_____

_____

6. Have you watched a friend, roommate, work, or school colleague waste their paycheck, bonus, allowance, inheritance, etc.? What did you think and how did watching this make you feel?

_____

_____

CHAPTER THREE

DEBAUCHERY AND MURPHY'S LAW

Now when he had spent everything, a severe famine occurred in that country, and he began to be impoverished. So he went and hired himself out to one of the citizens of that country, and he sent him into his fields to feed swine. And he would have gladly filled his stomach with the pods that the swine were eating, and no one was giving anything to him. But when he came to his senses, he said, "How many of my father's hired men have more than enough bread, but I am dying here with hunger! I will get up and go to my father, and will say to him, 'Father, I have sinned against heaven, and in your sight; I am no longer worthy to be called your son; make me as one of your hired men'"

(Luke 15:14-19 NASB).

"Anything that can go wrong will go wrong."[3] This is Murphy's Law. Maybe you've experienced a few seasons in your life when this seemed to be true. I've had my share of times when it seemed as though everything was going bad, all at the same time. My kids were sick, our car broke down, we got an unexpected bill, I received bad news from a family member,

I had a hurtful conversation with a friend, and we had financial pressures, deadlines, health challenges, etc. During one of these seasons, I remember thinking, *What can I focus on that won't make me upset!?*

In the Prodigal Son parable, we read that the younger son squandered his inheritance and ran out of money in a foreign country. In the previous chapter, we explored what it meant culturally that the son asked for his inheritance prematurely, and we watched his decision to move away and party. He partied so hard that he burned through his inheritance and had nothing to show for his choices.

He lost his fair-weather friends and had nothing left when a famine hit the country. In this foreign country, with no money, no friends, no resources, and experiencing famine, what could this man do?

It seems to be the perfect storm for the younger son, since all of his wealth is gone at the same time the country is experiencing a famine: Murphy's Law. It seems as if there's only one thing for the younger son to do and that is to *join* himself to a citizen in that country.

The Greek verb that is used to communicate joining is the word κολλάω. This is an interesting word because it means "to glue or adhere, intimately connected in a soul-knit friendship."[4] It doesn't imply a transactional relationship, like getting paid for doing work or bartering to exchange services for food or lodging. This is not a cause-and-effect verb, but more like an attaching or connecting. What we see through the use of this verb is that the younger son connected to the citizen in hopes of getting something (food, lodging, safety, protection, etc.), but it wasn't a mutually agreed upon relationship.

> *The younger son connected to the citizen in hopes of getting something, but it wasn't a mutually agreed upon relationship.*

I often travel internationally for the work I do with Saving Moses, a nonprofit that I started that saves babies by meeting the most urgent and intense survival needs where help is least available. The countries where we work are very poor, and it's not unusual when we drive places around a large city and come to a stop that we are swarmed with people washing the windows, shining the car, cleaning the headlights and more, all in hopes of getting a few coins from us before the light turns green and we drive away. It's this kind of action that gives some modern context to the *joining* that the younger son did with the citizen in the foreign country. He joins himself to the citizen, hoping to have some kind of help or support.

As a result of this joining, the younger son is sent into the citizen's field to feed his pigs. Remember that Jesus is telling this parable to a Jewish audience. Because of the ban that the Law gave to Jewish folks regarding associating with pigs, they (especially the religious leaders listening) would be repulsive and highly offended to hear that the younger son associated with pigs. Nevertheless, the younger son is left to feed pigs. We read in verse 16, "And he would have gladly filled his stomach with the pods that the swine were eating, and no one was giving *anything* to him."

Family Insight

My name is Francine, and I'm the oldest of the two daughters my parents raised. Since my dad was in the military throughout my childhood, we moved a lot. By the time I was twelve years old, we had moved five times, including being stationed in Germany when I was toddler. Most people think that moving so often made it difficult for me to have friends, but I found ways to cultivate friendships during my upbringing, and I have a few lifelong friends to this day, whom I love deeply.

In relation to my parents, my father was a tank systems maintainer in the Army and my mom worked in the home during my elementary school years. My dad was extremely quiet, never raised his voice, and always maintained a steady demeanor. He was a man of few words and no affection. When he worked all day, he came home and worked on projects in and around the house. His interactions with my sister and me were giving directions and instructions but nothing more. My mom affirmed our interests and generally let natural consequences be the feedback for our choices rather than yelling, spanking, or employing strict rules. She made sure that we had transportation to all our activities and regular meals at home. Our dinner times were fairly quiet and without tension or conflicts.

In third grade, I began taking saxophone lessons, and this became my main interest throughout my schooling, outside of my academic achievements, which were very important to me. For my academic achievements, I never received compliments or accolades from my parents, but I was highly internally motivated to get good grades and straight As. In addition to saxophone lessons, I taught myself other wind instruments and joined a variety of bands from elementary school through part of my university studies. I was part of the marching band, symphonic band, jazz band, concert band, and all things band.

While I was always busy with band practices and performances, I found my closest friendships from our church attendance every Sunday, which usually lasted almost all day. These friendships were really great for me, and some of them have remained with me for more than four decades.

Because I was a fairly sensitive child, it didn't take much to correct me or for me to align with my parents' wishes and desires. My parents didn't raise their voices, nor were they heavy disciplinarians. They also didn't demand high achievements from me. Maybe that's because I was strongly motivated within myself. To that end, I worked hard to get full-ride scholarships to college and carve out a career for myself from my Bachelor of Science in Math.

While Francine's "Family Insight" doesn't have an explicit Murphy's Law experience, it's helpful, nonetheless, to have this insight into her upbringing. In relation to our parable, let's remember that the son is living in a foreign country, which means he doesn't have resources available to him that would have been available in his own country. His party friends didn't stick around to help him, nor is he a citizen in this country. Consequently, he's detached from community support, like his home village. He is basically a homeless vagrant. Furthermore, he has partied away all of his money, so he's not able to "buy" any friendship.

On top of all this, the country where he's living begins to experience a famine, so people there are less inclined to be charitable and generous. From what we read about the foreign citizen to whom our son joined himself, it appears that he's not very helpful. I make this observation because he doesn't give the younger son any food. Indeed, no one gives him any food. He gets so hungry that he's inclined to eat the pig slop that he's giving to the pigs. We read that he would have gladly filled his stomach with the pods the pigs were eating, but no one gave him anything.

What could pig slop look like at this time? In the simplest definition, pig slop is made up of everything that's waste from a kitchen: corn cobs, sour milk, spoiled fruits and veggies, egg shells, food scraps, peels from fruits and veggies, onion tops, etc. Generally, whatever the humans didn't eat was given to the pigs for slop. This son was so hungry that he wanted to eat the pig food, but this wasn't available to him.

> *What the younger son is experiencing is due to his choices.*

The convergence of all these bad things seems to be the quintessential Murphy's Law, except for this noteworthy consideration: what the younger son is experiencing is due to his choices. These are the choices that this son made:

- He dishonored his dad.
- He packed up all his stuff and took his inheritance.
- He moved to a foreign country.
- In that country, he squandered his inheritance on frivolous living.

Family Insight

My name is Sophia, and my parents have three children: my brother who is eight years older than me, and my little brother who is four years younger than me. My mom told me that she and dad had tried for quite some time to have children, hence the long gaps in the ages between my siblings and me. Because there's such a big age difference between my brother and me, I kind of grew up as an only child, until my little brother came along.

Before he came on the scene, I played with my mom all the time—dolls, make-believe castles, decorating cookies, planting flowers, baking zucchini bread, and dressing up as beauty queens. We also got our nails done, and I loved when she'd fix up my hair with the curling iron, hair spray, and rollers.

As for my dad, he seemed to be mostly occupied with his job, my older brother's athletic competitions, and watching baseball on TV in the summer. I also remember my dad teaching my brother about changing the oil in his car because the oil stain in the garage from dad's lesson never disappeared, even though my mom scrubbed it for a long time.

She wasn't happy about the stain, which made sense to me because we routinely cleaned the house and worked hard to keep it orderly and tidy. My dad and older brother, not so much. Sometimes, this was a point of contention, but mostly my family was pretty happy and kind to each other.

When I started school, I totally loved it! I earned good grades, and I was often the teacher's pet. In elementary school, we had a theater / drama class, which is where I discovered my joy in acting and singing. Whenever there was an opportunity to act, join a play, sing, or perform, I'd do my best to audition for a part, or at least be on the support crew for any production.

The biggest hurt in my upbringing was when my family would make snide comments about people in the LGBTQ community while watching a TV show, movie, or seeing one of "them" at a school event. I found their comments to be extremely hurtful, and their posture made it all the more difficult to let them know I'm a lesbian, which I did in my early 20s. By this point, my older brother had his own home and was established in his business career. My younger brother was finishing up high school, so the conversations in the family were initially stressful around the subject of my identity. After some time, everyone figured out how to be settled with me, and I'm grateful to have loving and supportive parents and brothers. I have several friends who don't have loving families, which makes me all the more thankful for mine.

The Help

Over the course of this parable, each of our main characters (the younger son, older son, and father) has important engagements with various servants, hirelings, and house help. We'll see how these various workers and supports helped each of the main characters in different ways.

Starting with the younger son, he remembers day workers who are engaged by his dad. This memory provides a stark contrast with his fully ravenous condition, which sparks an idea in his mind. At this position of rock bottom, the son has an epiphany. The Greek uses the phrase, "he came to himself." In this epiphany, the son reflects on life at his home where the *hired hands* have more than enough bread to eat. The word in the Greek that is used for *hired hands* is the word μίσθιος (mis-thios), and it means "a paid worker, hired servant, hireling."[5] This is a person who does a job and gets paid (food) for doing the job.

As we consider the reflection of the younger son, we see that he was aware of not only his home life, but the people who were hired by his dad. He knew how his dad treated these workers or hirelings. There were provisions and fair payment for the household laborers.

The younger son works out a plan so that he can get food in exchange for being a day laborer for his dad. No doubt, he would have to humble himself and accept that his actions and words to his father at the beginning of the story postured him no longer to be a son in his father's family. Additionally, he would have to suffer the outrage and rejection from his village for his dishonorable behaviors, never mind showing up with his emaciated, smelly, ugly, dirty, and scantily clothed body.

It seems to be that when we are at our lowest point, we often have clarity about the decisions that we must make. Maybe we feel all the lack, discomfort, hunger, shame, isolation, pain, and misery when we hit rock bottom. Such realizations can facilitate powerful motivations to get away from our painful reality. There are no shortages of examples of people who found themselves at the bottom of their life and made powerful decisions to get away from that bottom.

It seems to be that when we are at our lowest point, we often have clarity about the decisions that we must make.

This reminds me of one of my friends who grew up in a fairly affluent family. She had lots of encouragement and resources to go to college and "make something of herself." When she graduated high school, she decided to do a gap year. A few decades later, she still wishes that she'd skipped this idea and went the college education route. Although she traveled the world, saw incredible sights, and enjoyed a wide range of experiences, many of her experiences were not so good.

When she came home from her gap year, she had lots of health struggles (because of STDs), she had a dependency on drugs, and her parents had to hire multiple exterminators to get rid of all the mites, bedbugs, chiggers, and vermin that she brought home with her. After a few months and lots of support with tearful conversations, my friend decided to go to a local HVAC trade school, get the training and a few years of experience in this profession that she needed. Today, she owns her own HVAC company and has let the lessons she learned after her gap year serve as reminders of "never going back to those dark days."

Similar to my friend, the younger son chose to humble himself when he hit the bottom. He repented and returned to his dad to ask to be a day laborer. He did this for the simple reason that he could count on eating every day as a hireling, rather than pining to eat pig slop that never materialized. Humility and bread were better than pigs, starvation, and isolation. I'd suggest that the younger son returned to his dad as a different person than the hurtful son who dishonored his dad and left home with his inheritance.

As we finish looking at the younger son, let's reflect on what he decided to say to his dad after he came to his senses. Here are a few translations to help you have a more colorful picture of this son's planned greeting with his dad:

> *Father, I have sinned against heaven and before you. I am no longer worthy to be called your son. Treat me as one of your hired servants* (ESV).

> *Father, I've sinned against God, I've sinned before you; I don't deserve to be called your son. Take me on as a hired hand* (MSG).

> *Father, I was wrong. I have sinned against you. I'll never again be worthy to be called your son. Please, Father, just treat me like one of your employees* (TPT).

It's important to note that the first word he planned to say was, "Father" implying family connection and position. Upon making this statement, he immediately acknowledges his wrongdoing and hurtful decisions, along with the loss of his position in the family. We can see from his words that the rock-bottom experience had recalibrated his thinking to recognize that he no longer deserved to be called "son." He had gone far beyond the point of no return with his dad, and he was painfully aware of this reality.

The Audience

As we finish our deep-dive exploring for the younger son in this parable, let's keep in mind who is listening to Jesus tell this parable. Remember that in Luke 15:1-2 we read that the sinners and tax collectors were coming to hear Jesus, while the religious leaders were complaining about such reprobates and losers. In this story, maybe Jesus was referring to the sinners and tax collectors when He described the younger brother, since he wasn't interested in being proper, righteous, or maintaining customary respect for his dad or inheritance.

Maybe you partied away your inheritance and squandered your resources with stupid choices. Maybe you live in the shame and loss of our decisions, and perhaps your regrets are weightier than your pleasures. If you relate to the younger son in this parable, be grateful that your Father's love can be the final solution rather than the ongoing hurt and humiliation from riotous living and poor choices.

CHAPTER THREE: DEBAUCHERY AND MURPHY'S LAW

R&R: Reflect and Respond

1. Think of a time in your life when everything seemed to go wrong. In the space provided, identify all the things that went wrong or fell apart in this season.

   _____

   _____

2. At that rock bottom, how many of the bad things were coincidental and how many were results of poor decisions you made?

   _____

   _____

3. What did you do at that rock bottom and how long did the rock bottom season last?

   _____

   _____

4. What were some things that helped you move beyond the rock bottom?

_____

_____

5. What are some lessons you learned from this season?

_____

_____

6. What are some scars you carry from this season?

_____

_____

7. How did this season change you?

_____

_____

PART TWO

THE OLDER SON

Then he said, "There was once a man who had two sons. The younger said to his father, 'Father, I want right now what's coming to me.' So the father divided the property between them. It wasn't long before the younger son packed his bags and left for a distant country. There, undisciplined and dissipated, he wasted everything he had. After he had gone through all his money, there was a bad famine all through that country and he began to hurt. He signed on with a citizen there who assigned him to his fields to slop the pigs. He was so hungry he would have eaten the corncobs in the pig slop, but no one would give him any. That brought him to his senses. He said, 'All those farmhands working for my father sit down to three meals a day, and here I am starving to death. I'm going back to my father. I'll say to him, Father, I've sinned against God, I've sinned before you; I don't deserve to be called your son. Take me on as a hired hand.' He got right up and went home to his father.

"When he was still a long way off, his father saw him. His heart pounding, he ran out, embraced him, and kissed him. The son started his speech: 'Father, I've sinned against God, I've sinned before you; I don't deserve to be called your son ever again.' But the father

wasn't listening. He was calling to the servants, 'Quick. Bring a clean set of clothes and dress him. Put the family ring on his finger and sandals on his feet. Then get a grain-fed heifer and roast it. We're going to feast! We're going to have a wonderful time! My son is here—given up for dead and now alive! Given up for lost and now found!' And they began to have a wonderful time.

"All this time his older son was out in the field. When the day's work was done he came in. As he approached the house, he heard the music and dancing. Calling over one of the houseboys, he asked what was going on. He told him, 'Your brother came home. Your father has ordered a feast—barbecued beef!—because he has him home safe and sound.' The older brother stalked off in an angry sulk and refused to join in. His father came out and tried to talk to him, but he wouldn't listen. The son said, 'Look how many years I've stayed here serving you, never giving you one moment of grief, but have you ever thrown a party for me and my friends? Then this son of yours who has thrown away your money on whores shows up and you go all out with a feast!' His father said, 'Son, you don't understand. You're with me all the time, and everything that is mine is yours—but this is a wonderful time, and we had to celebrate. This brother of yours was dead, and he's alive! He was lost, and he's found!'" (Luke 15:11-32 MSG)

CHAPTER FOUR

PROPER PIETY AND DUTIFUL COMPLIANCE

And He said, "A man had two sons"

(Luke 15:11 NASB).

Have you ever heard of the concept of birth order? There's lots of content written and presented around this theme and the characteristics that are often associated with one's birth order in a family. In general terms, for example, people often think that the oldest kid in a family tends to be the most responsible and dutiful. The firstborn can often demonstrate leadership qualities, be a high achiever, and have a superior posture in relation to their siblings.[6]

I had a brother who was almost eight years older than me. While I was technically the youngest sibling, I exhibited lots of the same characteristics normally attributed to firstborn children. I was responsible and strove to get good grades. I set high goals for myself and was very compliant and dutiful. While my brother was the oldest sibling, he didn't conform to whole birth-order theory, as he didn't care about his grades very much and he didn't pay much attention to the dutiful compliance norm for being the eldest child. So much for modern wisdom and cookie-cutter stereotypes!

In spite of the fact that my brother and I ran against customary thinking, the theories around birth order are well documented. As for biblical times, there are some commonalities and overlaps that we can observe, but there are also some interesting differences. Consequently, it's very important and useful to get some awareness around the social norms and expectations for the firstborn or oldest son in a family during Jesus' day.

Culture and History

In biblical times, the oldest son held a very significant position in the family. To begin with, the oldest son was seen as the first evidence of a father's strength. The firstborn was entitled to the birthright and a special blessing from the father. Consider Isaac and his sons (Esau and Jacob) in Genesis 25–28 to see a powerful narrative on the traditions and culture around the firstborn in a family about five thousand years ago.

When Jesus told the Prodigal Son parable, probably two thousand years after Jacob and Esau, the role of the eldest son had expanded in significant ways. The firstborn son was considered to be the father's right hand. This son was an extension of his father, representing his dad and the best interests of the family, speaking on behalf of his dad, personifying family values, and co-hosting family events and parties.

It's also interesting to consider that the oldest son had the responsibility to mediate between his dad and whatever conflict might arise, within the family as well as the surrounding community. If someone in the village had an argument or falling out with his dad or a family member, the oldest son had the task of trying to mediate and intervene for resolution and favorable outcomes. For all practical purposes, the oldest son had the position that was closest to his dad, looking out for the best interests of the family, its wealth and reputation, and protecting the family from hurtful possibilities. We could say that the oldest son was in training to take over the family leadership once the father passed away.

> *The oldest son was in training to take over the family leadership once the father passed away.*

In thinking about the roles and responsibilities of the oldest son, let's remember Jesus' first words about this interesting family: "A man had two sons" (Luke 15:11). And immediately, Jesus steps into the tension that's caused from the younger son's request to receive his portion of the inheritance. This request would create tremendous strain and a rift between the younger son and his dad.

Given that it was the oldest son's responsibility to mediate conflicts for his dad, it's interesting to note that the older son didn't step in to mediate the rift between his dad and brother. While this was the cultural norm at this time, the older son is conspicuously missing.

In customary behaviors, the older son would have had separate conversations with his brother and father, attempting to sort out the conflict and find an agreeable conclusion. So immediately, the audience listening to Jesus' parable would ask questions about the older son not taking on his responsibility to mediate the painful rift within his family. Where is the older son? Either this son is awkwardly quiet or uncharacteristically absent. Clearly, the younger son highly offended his dad, but the older son did nothing to resolve the conflict or assuage his father's pain.

In terms of being his father's right hand, this older son fell short in the first verses of this parable. Furthermore, there's no mention of this son until the last half of the parable. Based on the cultural norms during the telling of this parable, Jesus' audience could have easily thought that the older son had failed in his responsibilities with his dad and family—missing in action.

Also, the inheritance request from the younger son would have had some impact on the inheritance of the older son. When their dad divided up the wealth between his sons, the older son acquired his inheritance. From the parable, we can assume that he stayed home with his wealth and maintained his position and work in the family. Nevertheless, the older son is curiously quiet and a non-entity in the first verses of this parable. He's a spectator at best but certainly not a participant in the hurtful conflict between his brother and father.

As Jesus moves through this parable, working through the actions of the younger son and the father's extravagant love to reconcile this son, we come to the verses that revolve around the older son. Starting in Luke 15:25 we read, "Now his older son was in the field, and when he came and approached the house, he heard music and dancing."

Family Insight

My name is Mary, and my family revolved around all things Bill Gothard. You could watch the "Shiny Happy People" docuseries for some insights on what the teachings of Bill Gothard could look like in a family context.

For a quick overview of Bill Gothard, he was born in Illinois in 1934. He earned his BA from Wheaton

University in Biblical Studies. In 1961, he founded Campus Teams, which was renamed to Institute in Basic Life Principles (IBLP). In 1984, Gothard founded the Advanced Training Institute (ATI), which created a homeschooling curriculum based on Jesus' Sermon on the Mount. Since homeschooling at this time was largely a new phenomenon in the US, many Christian families quickly signed up for the ATI curriculum to educate their kids in biblical principles and to protect their kids from satanic and worldly influences.

My parents enrolled us (my three sisters and two brothers) in this curriculum, and I was homeschooled for all my education through high school. In this curriculum, I learned about the "umbrella of authority," such that I understood that I was only safe when I stayed under the umbrella of my dad's authority first and then my mom's authority. To this end, we didn't leave the house much, except to attend church. We wore ultra-conservative clothes, there was no TV in our home until I was seventeen years old, and I didn't have any friends to speak of beyond my family.

In relation to my homelife, my mom was very supportive and nurturing. She loved God, and she loved her husband and her kids. She almost always deferred to my dad's choices because she was a good Christian wife, very submissive. My dad was a strong authoritarian and could struggle with anger issues. Dinnertime wasn't enjoyable because usually a fight broke out between my dad and one or a few of my siblings.

From the way I was raised and taught, I knew I was supposed to get married and have kids. However, the marriage thing didn't happen for me straight out of high school, not until I was in my early 20s. In the meantime, I decided to get my Bachelor's degree in Christian Ministry so that I could use my life to bring glory to God through ministry.

Thankfully, I now have been married for more than twenty years, and I have four wonderful children, each uniquely gifted and wholly wonderful. My kids have attended public school, and I've been happy to walk that journey with each of them, going through lumps and bumps while watching them grow, being deeply fulfilled to see them mature. I look back on my upbringing with the Bill Gothard control as largely hurtful, shaming, and fear-inducing. I made the choice from my convictions and experiences not to do this to my kids, to the best of my abilities.

The Party

In returning to our parable, let's think about the party experience for the older son and how this could relate to us. Did you ever experience a party happening at your house to which you were not invited? Did your parent(s) throw a party and make arrangements for you to spend the night at a friend's house during their party? Was there ever a spontaneous celebration at your house that caught you by surprise?

Did you ever experience a party happening at your house to which you were not invited?

It's interesting to read this verse in Luke about the older son being in the field and making his way to the house, only to hear dancing and music as he approached. In light of the culture at this time, we can imagine that the older son should have been at his father's side for whatever party was happening, as was the custom. He would have welcomed guests and been a secondary host and support to his dad. The older son would have watched for how he could help his dad to ensure that the party was going according to his dad's desires. But in Jesus' story, this son was in the field. There was a party at his house, and he didn't know about it. No wonder he asked a *houseboy* what the music, noise, and dancing was about.

The Help

In Luke 15:26 it says, "And he summoned one of the servants and began inquiring what these things could be." Let's look at the word for *servant* that is used in Luke 15:26. The word in Greek is παις (pais). Most English translations use the word *servant*; however, this word often denotes a slave, servant, or houseboy.[7] This is different than the hireling that the first son remembers. The attendant, παις, is not a day laborer, but rather a young boy or servant who worked around the house of someone who was often wealthy. This houseboy is the one who answered the older son as we read in verse 27, "And he said to him, 'Your brother has come, and your father has killed the fattened calf because he has received him back safe and sound.'"

In thinking about the interaction between the houseboy and the older son, let's also recall that the younger son remembered how the day workers for his dad had enough bread to eat. The memories of how his dad treated the day workers gave the younger son the idea about going home and becoming another hireling. The house servant gives the older son the *information* about the party that's happening at his house, while the recollection of the day workers at the younger son's home gave him the *inspiration* to return home.

Family Insight

My name is Cole, and I have a younger sister and many wonderful cousins. We are all really close in age, and I grew up with my cousins being every bit of family as my sister. Our grandparents also lived nearby and were very devoted and caring. My cousins, sister, and I are all very close in age, so we played together all the time. We went on vacations, had lots of birthday parties, and most importantly, celebrated life together!

It was very shocking to learn that when my sister was born, she was deaf. Of course, that's been a journey for my family to navigate, as we learned how to communicate with her and give her support that was helpful to her. I've always felt a close bond with her, and I've endeavored to be her biggest advocate, after my mom and dad.

My parents were incredible throughout my upbringing, being supportive with both of us and our unique interests. In elementary school, we all played various instruments, joined science clubs, competed in sports, and routinely visited the library. I attribute my voracious appetite to read from our regular library visits and getting my own library card when I was really young.

My sister is an incredible soccer player, and I'm certain that the continual support of our parents has been an integral reason for her success. Some of this success included earning a full-ride scholarship to university to play for their soccer team.

I was more artistically inclined and discovered a love for acting when I was in middle school. I tried out for the school play and discovered a zeal for all things thespian and theater. Naturally, my parents supported my interest and applauded the loudest at all of my performances and plays throughout all of my schooling. I always felt their love and support for me and never questioned their deep care and steady presence in my life.

Since we regularly attended temple, as my parents are devout Mormons, it was really challenging and a massive struggle when I let my family know that I'm gay. This was around the time when I was finishing up high school. There was no shortage of conversations with my parents, sister, and extended family around my sexuality. For a little while, there was lots of tension and misunderstandings. However, my parents have always been loving and supportive of me and my sister. As such, they made it clear that their love for me wouldn't change, regardless of my identity. It was also deeply fulfilling to have my grandfather officiate my wedding with my wonderful husband.

Some of my extended family, however, haven't been as supportive as my parents. They have chosen to stay polite, but aloof. Of course, I'm sad about this, and I hope that my relationships with them will change and soften in the future. If there was one value that I carry away from my upbringing, it's the value of compassion and support. This value was demonstrated to me consistently throughout my childhood.

Returning to our parable and thinking about the help, both the day laborers and the houseboy are the conduits for these sons to connect with their home and father. We would be wise to recognize that even the most revered Christian leader is nothing but a servant to point us back to our Heavenly Father and living as a son or daughter. Let's never escalate servants to be more important than our Father.

Even the most revered Christian leader is nothing but a servant to point us back to our Heavenly Father.

Once the older son heard the explanation of the celebration from the houseboy, he was angry and refused to join the party. Why was he angry? At the first blush, he might have been angry because he wasn't included or invited. There was a party happening at his house, and no one had come to the field to invite him to join the party. In that sense, he could have been angry because he felt rejected or excluded. I don't doubt that these were pieces that contributed to his anger.

At the same time, once the older son heard about the party and the return of his younger brother, he did not immediately rush to the house to figure out how he could best support his dad. Given what was customary and dutiful in this culture, the older son missed some very key roles and responsibilities in his firstborn son position. He neglected to mediate the rift between his little brother and his dad. Furthermore, when there was a grand welcome-home party for his brother, he chose to stay in the field rather than hustle to his dad's side to be a support and a co-host with his dad. So much for dutiful compliance and familial support!

So much for dutiful compliance and familial support!

The next chapter will help us unpack all the ingredients that went into the anger of the older son.

CHAPTER FOUR: PROPER PIETY AND DUTIFUL COMPLIANCE

R&R: Reflect and Respond

1. Do you have siblings? Where are you in the birth order of your family?

_____

_____

2. In relation to seeing yourself as God's son or daughter, do you relate more to the younger or older son?

_____

_____

3. Have there been occasions when you have seen someone in your church or family making poor decisions, but you chose to keep your distance?

_____

_____

4. What do you think and how do you feel about the absence and silence of the older son?

_____

_____

5. Did you ever have family responsibilities that you didn't fulfill? What might some of these have been? What was your reasoning for not doing these things?

_____

_____

CHAPTER FIVE

COMPARISON AND UNFAIRNESS

But he became angry and was not willing to go in; and his father came out and began pleading with him
(Luke 15:28 NASB).

This verse always makes me think of a pouty kid not getting his or her way while a loving and patient parent tries to engage his or her child with grace. It's one thing to watch a two-year-old have a tantrum over a candy, but it's an entirely different scenario to see a full-grown man do the pouty, grumpy dance because he feels slighted. If I was in his shoes, maybe I would have the same reaction.

Let's look at what the older son says to his dad in Luke 15:29-30 (NASB):

But he answered and said to his father, "Look! For so many years I have been serving you and I have never neglected a command of yours; and yet you have never given me a young goat, so that I might celebrate with my friends; but when this son of yours came, who has devoured your wealth with prostitutes, you killed the fattened calf for him."

There's a whole lot of emotions to unpack in the older son's reply. For starters, he doesn't speak to his dad by the term "father" or "dad." This is noteworthy, because it's a contrast with the beginning of the younger son's engagement with his dad, upon returning from the pig feeding and party disaster. Upon meeting his dad, the first word of the younger son is, "Father." In contrast, the older son greets his dad with the word, "Look!" or "Behold!"

The party son who sees himself as unworthy greets his dad with, "Father." The pious son who thinks that he's deserving and worthy doesn't address his dad in any relational context. Instead, he demands that his dad look at his achievements, piety, and dutiful compliance. "Look!"

The pious son who thinks that he's deserving and worthy doesn't address his dad in any relational context.

Furthermore, he makes it clear that he feels slighted by his dad when he brings up the party with the fattened calf and the absence of a party with a young goat. Let's think for a few minutes about what the older son is saying to his dad, looking at a few different translations to get the full experience of the emotions in Luke 15:29:

All these years I've slaved for you and never once refused to do a single thing you told me to. And in all that time you never gave me even one young goat for a feast with my friends (NLT).

But he answered his father, "Look! All these years I've been slaving for you and never disobeyed your orders.

Yet you never gave me even a young goat so I could celebrate with my friends" (NIV).

The son said, "Father, listen! How many years have I worked like a slave for you, performing every duty you've asked as a faithful son? And I've never once disobeyed you. But you've never thrown a party for me because of my faithfulness. Never once have you even given me a goat that I could feast on and celebrate with my friends as this son of yours is doing now" (TPT).

Look! For so many years I have been serving you and I have never neglected a command of yours; and yet you have never given me a young goat, so that I might celebrate with my friends (NASB).

We can easily see his position of righteous indignation. "I've served you. I followed all of your directives and commands. I'm deserving because of my actions. I dotted all the 'Is' and crossed all the 'Ts.' I've earned my position, and I deserve to be compensated. But instead, my loser brother is getting the party of a lifetime, and I'm out here in the field being slighted, ignored, and excluded!"

"I've earned my position, and I deserve to be compensated. But instead, my loser brother is getting the party of a lifetime."

Family Insight

My name is Thor, and I grew up in a blended family with two stepbrothers and one stepsister. I was the solo offspring from my parents as my half siblings came from the previous marriages of my parents.

My parents continue to be my heroes well into my adulthood, and they serve as role models for me as I father my own kids. As I think about my childhood, it was filled with adventure, exploring a wide array of interests from football to oboe, karate to Boy Scouts, and anything that might appeal to me. Additionally, my parents had two non-negotiables in my growing up years. The first non-negotiable was that I would always have plenty of books. They recognized when I was little that I had a voracious appetite to read, and they ensured that I never ran short on books. I read all kinds of books like *The Hardy Boys, Goosebumps* series, and everything that Stephen King wrote. Throughout all my life, I've been a reader, and I attribute this to my parents supporting my reading interest from its inception.

The second non-negotiable with my parents is that I would always have clothes that fit me. This has always been a big issue, because I've always been a physically big person. I know that I inherited this from my dad because he was a massive man, seeing that he was 6 feet 3 inches and 240 pounds. In addition to his physical size, he had a giant personality, overflowing with laughter and love for people. This is probably why he was such a successful employee with FEMA (Federal Emergency

Management Agency) and why hundreds of people attended his funeral. His laugh was infectious, and he treated everyone with the utmost kindness. He was a hard worker and made sure to attend all of my games, matches, recitals, etc. Unfortunately, he died too soon, and I miss him every day.

My mom made sure to help us get up in the morning and ready for school. She was a home healthcare worker who worked nightshifts, and she has a heart of gold. She is naturally nurturing and looks after lots of practical needs, like meals, laundry, transportation, etc. Growing up, both of my parents were present every day, even though they worked full time and had heavy employment responsibilities. I could summarize the investments my parents put in me by saying that I have my strength from my dad and my heart from my mom. I am who I am today because of my wonderful, loving, supportive, and nurturing parents!

In returning to our parable, let's remember that the older son didn't step into the customary roles and responsibilities to mediate and reconcile the broken relationship between his dad and brother at the beginning of the parable. But in the final conversation with his dad, he's heralding his service and pious obedience to his dad. There's some hypocrisy to what this son is saying in contrast to what he's done.

None of the things the older son claims that he did expresses relationship, family, or connection with his dad. At the beginning of the parable, the older son is missing, and at the end of the parable, he's offended and hostile, to the point of excluding himself from the welcome-home party for his little brother.

Clearly, there's not much relationship between the older son and his dad. This is the choice of the older son, because we see that it is the father who goes out to him trying to bring connection and relationship.

> *None of the things the older son claims that he did expresses relationship, family, or connection with his dad.*

The Party

Let's think for a moment about the party or celebration theme from the perspective of the older son. In his angry answer to his dad—in the middle of refusing to attend a party for his reconciled brother—this son brings up how he never got to have a party with his friends. Instead of celebrating with his family and embracing his father's values, the older son expressed how he felt cheated by not getting to celebrate with his friends. He rejected the values of his father. This son would rather pout and be angry away from his home and disconnected from his dad instead of celebrating with his community and welcoming his lost brother. No doubt that his words and overall posture toward his dad hurt immensely.

Family Insight

My name is Jenny, and I grew up in Michigan with my mom, spending part of my summers with my dad in California. They were married until I was about three years old. It was at this age when my mom cut off access for my dad to be around his kids. He's an alcoholic, and mom felt that my brother and I would be safer if we moved away from him to where he couldn't find us. This was what she told us, but once my dad's new wife tracked us down, he pressed the legal requirements so that we could visit him a few times a year.

To be clear, I loved getting time with my dad. Truly, he's my knight in shining armor, and visiting him was the highlight for me each year. My dad, despite being an alcoholic, is loving, supportive, kind, affirming, and strong.

My mom, on the other hand, is not these things. Truly, she was most happy when I was most miserable, and I grew up as a scapegoat child. This means that I got the blame for everything bad, and I received no validation or support for my achievements or interests. She continually shamed me, physically and verbally abused me, and withheld food as a form of punishment.

I desperately wanted her affection and validation, so I worked overtime to get good grades and be worthy to earn her support, which I didn't receive. I learned very quickly that telling anyone about my struggles would backfire at home on me, with mom shaming, grounding, punishing, and doing awful things. Keeping a shiny, happy pretense ensured that my home existence didn't go beyond hellish.

Additionally, we moved frequently, so I never had stable friends and didn't have the opportunity to flourish in sports, clubs, student government, etc. We also were poor, so if I wanted to play sports or do anything extracurricular, I had to come up with the money on my own, which means I had my first job when I was thirteen years old.

My mom worked as an executive administrative assistant for a variety of companies, including various educational contexts. At one point, she was the executive assistant for the headmaster of a boarding school where I was forced to attend. She thought it was a fantastic idea so that I'd have a place to live and have steady food. When word got out among the students about my mom being the assistant to the headmaster, things went south for me at the school. Consequently, I was relieved when we moved, yet again.

From my upbringing, I learned to be a really hard worker, to be self-reliant, and to create the veneer of being happy and solicitous. As an adult, I'm learning to pay attention to my inner child and let her experience compassion, support, and healing.

Is it possible that we diminish our Heavenly Father's attempts to reconcile and connect with us? Is it possible that we're working hard to earn our place? Is it possible that we are jealous of someone around us? Might we be hurt and refuse to let our Father's comfort, affection, and invitations be the dominant voice and paradigm in our hearts?

Might we be hurt and refuse to let our Father's comfort, affection, and invitations be the dominant voice and paradigm in our hearts?

More than once, I have been the older son, striving to be worthy, endeavoring to be pious, and laboring to belong. I've seen more than a few undeserving people come to Jesus and receive our Father's welcome and celebration only for me to be cranky and surly. If we find ourselves looking down on people, those who are different from us, individuals who aren't devout followers of Jesus or righteous and upstanding citizens, it is possible that we are stepping into the shoes of the older brother. Is it our position or right to tell people who is and who is not God's beloved child? This is what the older brother did, and Jesus concludes the parable with the older son still separated from the celebration and possibly hostile with his dad.

The perspective of the older son is that he earned, he deserved, he achieved his status and rightful compensation. But his perspective and expressed values were not family, nor did they reflect connection or attachment with his dad. This is true from the beginning of the parable when he's silent and missing and at the end when he is accusatory and hostile in his engagement with his father. The older son, despite his perceived piety, is missing in action with anything family. He's missing at the beginning of the parable, and he's missing at the family party to celebrate his brother's return.

The Audience

As we wrap up this chapter, let's remember that two groups of people are hearing this parable: the reprobates (sinners and tax collectors) and the righteous (Pharisees and scribes). I wonder what went through the thoughts and feelings of the righteous group when they heard the conversation between the father and the older son? Did they see themselves in this parable? Was there some reflection about the sinners, tax collectors, and "younger brothers"?

Indeed, we would be wise to think about the possibility that we could be this older son from time to time. As I think about this for myself, reflecting on various seasons and times in my life, I can definitely see myself in this older son. There have been seasons in my life when my righteous piety was more important to me than an intimate connection with my Heavenly Father. There are also times in my life when I've been more like 70 percent younger son and 30 percent older son, sometimes the other way around as well.

We could be this older son from time to time.

I would suggest that one of the greatest values in this parable is to think about who we are in the three main characters, along with who we want to be. The central fulcrum is who we are with our Heavenly Father, because the father in this parable is the pivot point around whom everything revolves and gets explored.

CHAPTER FIVE:
COMPARISON AND UNFAIRNESS

R&R: Reflect and Respond

1. Describe a time when you felt left out, an outsider, or excluded from a celebration or party.

_____

_____

2. Describe a time when you felt highly justified for having righteous indignation.

_____

_____

3. How do you feel and what do you think when you read these words from the older son, "Look! For so many years I have been serving you and I have never neglected a command of yours."

_____

_____

4. If you had to choose between being more aligned with the younger son or the older son, who would you most relate to over the course of your life?

_____

_____

5. How do you feel about the son who is most unlike you?

_____

_____

PART THREE

THE FATHER

Jesus continued: "A man had two sons. The younger son told his father, 'I want my share of your estate now before you die.' So his father agreed to divide his wealth between his sons. A few days later this younger son packed all his belongings and moved to a distant land, and there he wasted all his money in wild living. About the time his money ran out, a great famine swept over the land, and he began to starve. He persuaded a local farmer to hire him, and the man sent him into his fields to feed the pigs. The young man became so hungry that even the pods he was feeding the pigs looked good to him. But no one gave him anything.

"When he finally came to his senses, he said to himself, 'At home even the hired servants have food enough to spare, and here I am dying of hunger! I will go home to my father and say, "Father, I have sinned against both heaven and you, and I am no longer worthy of being called your son. Please take me on as a hired servant."' So he returned home to his father. And while he was still a long way off, his father saw him coming. Filled with love and compassion, he ran to his son, embraced him, and kissed him. His son said to him, 'Father, I have sinned against both heaven and you, and I am no longer

worthy of being called your son.' But his father said to the servants, 'Quick! Bring the finest robe in the house and put it on him. Get a ring for his finger and sandals for his feet. And kill the calf we have been fattening. We must celebrate with a feast, for this son of mine was dead and has now returned to life. He was lost, but now he is found.' So the party began.

"Meanwhile, the older son was in the fields working. When he returned home, he heard music and dancing in the house, and he asked one of the servants what was going on. 'Your brother is back,' he was told, 'and your father has killed the fattened calf. We are celebrating because of his safe return.' The older brother was angry and wouldn't go in. His father came out and begged him, but he replied, 'All these years I've slaved for you and never once refused to do a single thing you told me to. And in all that time you never gave me even one young goat for a feast with my friends. Yet when this son of yours comes back after squandering your money on prostitutes, you celebrate by killing the fattened calf!' His father said to him, 'Look, dear son, you have always stayed by me, and everything I have is yours. We had to celebrate this happy day. For your brother was dead and has come back to life! He was lost, but now he is found!'" (Luke 15:11-32 NLT)

CHAPTER SIX

A FATHER'S PAIN AND REJECTION

And He said, "A man had two sons. The younger of them said to his father, 'Father, give me the share of the estate that falls to me.' So he divided his wealth between them"
(Luke 15:11-12 NASB).

Having children has been one of the most wonderful experiences in my life. It's also been the most challenging, humbling, prayer-inducing, perplexing, and growing journey ever. I love being a mom, and I deeply love each of my kids. I love their individuality, their different ways of looking at and doing life, I love their humor, zest for life, intelligence, compassion, strength, and wisdom. Over the course of time, as each of my kids has done his or her individual maturation journeys, I've been hurt by some of their choices.

It's not difficult for me to see how the father in this parable would be hurt by the words and choices of his younger son. But before we look at these interactions from the father's viewpoint, let's consider who the father is and what the cultural assumptions and filters were for the Jewish audience listing to Jesus tell this parable.

Culture and History

In Jesus' time, the father of a household was the leader in the family. He was responsible for protecting his family, for providing its wealth, for curating their social position, and for producing offspring to continue the family lineage and keep a secure future in all ways. The father, also known as *abba*, often had strong relationships with his kids, especially with his first-born son. When we think of fathers in the Bible, consider a few examples:

- Abraham and his two sons, Ishmael and Isaac. It's clear that Abraham had strong affections for each of his sons, considering these verses: for Ishmael, read Genesis 17:18, 21:10-11, and for Isaac, read Genesis 22:2.
- Jacob had Reuben and Joseph. Reuben is written about in Genesis 49:4, and Joseph is written about in Genesis 37:3. You can also read about Jacob's deep affection for his sons with his struggles around Benjamin going to Egypt during a severe regional famine in Genesis 42:36-38.
- David had many challenges with his kids, including Absalom who tried to depose his dad from his throne: 2 Samuel 13, 18:5, and 33.

Fathers were highly regarded and often considered the public face of the family. They often had very strong connections with at least a few of their kids, and it wasn't uncommon for people to think that God had smiled on a father who had lots of kids. Consider the psalmist's words in Psalm 127:3-5 (NASB): "Behold, children are a gift of the Lord, the fruit of the womb is a reward. Like arrows in the hand of a warrior, so are the children of one's youth. How blessed is the man whose quiver is full of them; they will not be ashamed when they speak with their enemies in the gate."

In the Prodigal Son parable, we can safely assume that the father was delighted to have two sons; however, when the younger son asked his father for his inheritance before his father's death or even illness, we can be very certain that this request massively hurt. Any father who was listening to Jesus tell the parable would have felt outraged on the fictional father's behalf. The younger son was basically saying that he wanted his dad dead so that he could have his inheritance. He wanted his dad's money more than his dad.

He wanted his dad's money more than his dad.

So what was inheritance like at this time and in this culture? Of course, there weren't stocks, bonds, trust accounts, or safety-deposit boxes. The development of our modern idea of currency didn't really become the common form of buying and selling until around AD 1000, even though there are plenty of ancient coins to show some of the development of our modern currency.

In Jesus' day, a family's wealth was wrapped up in livestock, land, gold, precious stones, jewelry, and maybe family heirlooms. In order to divide up the inheritance between his boys, the father would have had to figure out equivalent values or trades for his wealth such that it could be divided and given to his sons. This is what the father did to respond to his younger son's demand. He liquidated his estate to divide it between his sons.

While the father's pain from the demand of the younger son seems obvious, his pain because of the absence of his older son isn't quite as obvious. As I mentioned previously, the older son had been expected to be at his dad's right hand and mediate conflicts between his dad and others—particularly his younger brother. The fact that the older son was totally missing in the exchange between his brother and his dad is noteworthy.

This is all the more alarming to consider when the younger son quickly liquidates his inheritance and leaves the family with zero intervention from the older son. I suspect that the older brother's inheritance would have been impacted by his little brother's demand, and it's possible that he would have resented this impact.

In all of these exchanges, no one is behaving consistently with the cultural or social norms. The younger son wholly disrespects his dad, the oldest son is absent, and the father agrees to give his younger son his inheritance. Jesus' audience would have noticed immediately that none of the main characters of the parable was acting as was to be expected. I can imagine that everyone listening to Jesus tell this parable was wholly perplexed at the respective behaviors of each of these key characters.

As Jesus continues, He describes the choices and results of the younger son in Luke 15:13-16 that ended in loss, shame, and starvation. The younger son returns to his dad as a broken and destitute son. Upon this son's return, the father does what is wholly unexpected. Truly, when I read what the father does in Luke 15:20, I'm unraveled. The quantity and quality of love expressed by the father is nothing but fully divine, as I don't think that we humans have such extravagant love in our hearts without God's help.

The quantity and quality of love expressed by the father is nothing but fully divine.

Consider this verse in a few translations:

So he got up and came to his father. But while he was still a long way off, his father saw him and felt compassion for him, and ran and embraced him and kissed him (NASB).

So he returned home to his father. And while he was still a long way off, his father saw him coming. Filled with love and compassion, he ran to his son, embraced him, and kissed him (NLT).

When he was still a long way off, his father saw him. His heart pounding, he ran out, embraced him, and kissed him (MSG).

From a long distance away, his father saw him coming, dressed as a beggar, and great compassion swelled up in his heart for his son who was returning home. The father raced out to meet him, swept him up in his arms, hugged him dearly, and kissed him over and over with tender love (TPT).

As I read the parable today, I find the father's actions toward his younger son to be astounding. It is even more wondrous when his actions are put into the culture and time of the parable's telling. Instead of being pious and aloof, even expressing offense at his son's disrespect, the father is exuberant and unrestrained in his enthusiastic welcome for his son. Instead of letting his pain direct his actions and emotions, the father lets his love and affection lead him to heartily embrace and affectionately kiss his son.

It's interesting to consider that at this time in history, people in positions of honor and leadership didn't normally run. Running would require them to hoist up their clothing (robes) and expose their legs. Exposing one's legs was distasteful and considered vulgar. Nevertheless, the father's affection for his son far exceeded his concerns for social norms and acceptable behaviors.

The father's affection for his son far exceeded his concerns for social norms and acceptable behaviors.

Let's also consider that the father saw his son from a distance and ran that distance to embrace and welcome his son. This is noteworthy because the villagers where his home was situated would have known about the younger son's disrespect toward his dad. These villagers would have reviled him with ugly words, hateful actions, and closed doors. Because the father ran to his "outcast" son, the son didn't have to suffer the rejection and abusive treatment from the villagers. The father bridged the gap so that his son wouldn't have to experience humiliation or the ugly and unkind words from the villagers.

Family Values

In thinking about the father's family values and treatment for this disrespectful son, it's helpful to see his actions in the demonstrated priorities. The father did everything to express *personal reconciliation* with his son. He ran to close the gap between them. When he reached his son, the father didn't begin a parental sermon or berate his son for the poor choices and disrespectful actions he did. Instead, he falls on his son's neck and kisses him. Personally, I don't think there's a more exuberant or forgiving picture for personal reconciliation than what is demonstrated by this father.

There was nothing from the father to communicate to this lost son that he was too smelly, dirty, disgusting, unworthy, undeserving, or too far beyond his father's love and passion. There's not a hint of disdain or hesitation in the father's actions and outpouring of love.

Let's look at the verbs that are associated with his actions, as they will help punctuate the strong feelings the father expressed. To help us work through these verbs, let's refresh our awareness of Luke 15:20 (NASB): "So he got up and came to his father. But while he was still a long way off, his father saw him and felt compassion for him, and ran and embraced him and kissed him."

Seeing:

The father saw his son from a distance. Was his dad watching for him? Did his dad anticipate his son's return? Did the dad glance toward the horizon and just happen to see his son walking home? Because this is a parable that Jesus is telling us, we can't say with certainty what this looked like.

Compassion:

We can say, however, that when the father saw his son, he wasn't angry, punitive, vengeful, hostile, or pious. Verse 20 says that the father felt *compassion*. The word for compassion in the Greek that is used here is σπλαγχνίζομαι (splagznizomai).[8] It is used twelve times in the New Testament, all in the Gospels. It has the sense of feeling deeply or viscerally, to yearn, have compassion, pity. Rather than letting anger, punishment, or revenge lead his actions, the father had kindness and affection in his heart. Compassion was the father's motive for all his subsequent actions.

> *Compassion was the father's motive for all his subsequent actions.*

Run:

Rather than stroll or saunter his way to his son, the father runs. This Greek word τρέχω (trecho)[9] means "to run or walk hastily" and carries the idea of rushing and moving as fast as possible. The father ran to his son, not being concerned about his dignity or honor, but about receiving his son who had been gone for a long time.

Embrace:

Greek translations say that the father "fell on his neck." This is the same phrase that's used in Acts 20:37 when the church at Ephesus was saying goodbye to Paul, knowing that they wouldn't see him again. In our parable, rather than being a goodbye, this embrace is the wholehearted welcome of the father, overflowing with compassion and affection for his long-lost son.

Kiss:

It's relatively common in the Middle East for men to greet each other with a kiss on the cheek. In our story, however, we need to think about all the father's actions. The kiss carried with it the full weight and intensity of the joyous welcome the dad felt for his returning son. Instead of a slap to the face for being hurtful and disrespectful, or shunning and humiliating the son, the father is fully cohesive in all his actions to welcome home his son.

The Help

After receiving such a heartfelt acceptance, the younger son launches into his planned speech, only to be interrupted by his dad before he could finish. The father's interruption sets up the second reconciliation that would immediately be needed in the house for his son. The father instructs the servants to put the best robe on his son, a ring on his finger, and sandals on his feet. The father not only demonstrated affection and reconciliation to his outcast son, but he commanded his servants to come in line with his values and appropriately dress his son. Through these actions, we see the father command *household reconciliation*.

Perhaps some of these servants and house help might have felt anger and hostility toward this son for how he treated his dad. The father's commands to these servants made it clear that there would be no hostility toward his reconciled son from the servants. The father set the tone for how the household help would treat the newly returned son. Furthermore, by putting the best robe on his son, a ring on his finger, and sandals on his feet, the father ensures that none of the shame of his son's past will be displayed or observable in the house or among the servants. The father's instructions posture this son to look as if he had never offended his dad or lived among pigs in a foreign country. We can see that the father is totally committed to see his lost son be fully reconciled in his house.

> *The father's instructions posture this son to look as if he had never offended his dad or lived among pigs in a foreign country.*

Celebration and Party

Finally, since the father knew that his village would customarily ostracize and berate his younger son, he commanded his servants to kill their best animal for eating to make a community celebration, since the fattened calf would provide an abundance of tasty meat. Such a party would circumvent the social norms and demand a *community reconciliation* for his formerly outcast son. The father again set the tone for how the community would behave toward his reconciled son by throwing such an extravagant party for his return.

The party was not organized with scarcity or begrudgingly. If that had been the case, the meal would have been less extravagant and the music and overflow would have been less exuberant. Indeed, sacrificing the fattened calf is similar to eating a prime ribeye steak that is overflowing with fat and flavor. At this time in history, the fattened calf was an animal that was purposefully looked after with time, careful feeding, and less exercise to ensure a fatty and tasty meal. The fattened calf was saved for special occasions.

As we will see in the next chapter, the father made sure that there was dancing and music at this welcome-home celebration for the long-lost son. The jubilant party was loud and inclusive because the father's acceptance for his lost son was opulent and overflowing with affection!

As a side observation, you may have noticed that these two chapters related to the father in our parable do not have Family Insight breakaways. I have purposely left the Family Insights out of these chapters because the father in this parable is representative of our Heavenly Father. To that end, I wanted us to move our focus away from flawed and frail humans so that we could give our whole attention to look at our Heavenly Father—who is all things perfect with no human equivalent. Even though our parents can have the best intentions, and you might have had incredible parents, they are nonetheless flawed humans. We would be wise and could experience phenomenal healing, reconciliation, bonding, and redemption by making some adjustments with how we view the role our parents played.

CHAPTER SIX:
A FATHER'S PAIN AND REJECTION

R&R: Reflect and Respond

1. What do you think about the father giving his younger son his inheritance prematurely?

_____

_____

2. What do you think about the older son failing to mediate between his brother and dad?

_____

_____

3. Among the actions that the father did when his son returned home, which verb most catches your attention and why?
   - See
   - Compassion
   - Run
   - Fall / Embrace
   - Kiss
   - Commands
   - Reconcile

_____

_____

4. How have you experienced your Heavenly Father running to you for reconciliation?

_____

_____

5. What do you think about the father in this parable humbling himself by running out to his son?

_____

_____

6. What stands out to you most about the father and his actions in this chapter?

_____

_____

CHAPTER SEVEN

THE FATHER'S WANTS AND FAMILY VALUES

But he became angry and was not willing to go in; and his father came out and began pleading with him. But he answered and said to his father, "Look! For so many years I have been serving you and I have never neglected a command of yours; and yet you have never given me a young goat, so that I might celebrate with my friends; but when this son of yours came, who has devoured your wealth with prostitutes, you killed the fattened calf for him." And he said to him, "Son, you have always been with me, and all that is mine is yours. But we had to celebrate and rejoice, for this brother of yours was dead and has begun to live, and was lost and has been found"

(Luke 15:28-32 NASB).

What do you do with a child who doesn't reflect the family values and keeps himself at a distance from everyone in the family? Do you let him keep doing his stuff? Do you challenge or confront his point of view? Do you pull away your support and affirmation as a hopeful wake-up call so that he makes appropriate adjustments? Is your relationship with this child transactional? When the child doesn't conform to your desires and directives, do you sever or severely curtail the relationship? Additionally, how do you parent a self-righteous child or a child who chooses different values than what you modeled and trained during their upbringing? What happens when a child's attitude and actions begin to affect other siblings or family members?

These are questions not only for parents, but also for teachers when they have students who don't make choices that reflect the classroom values. They could also be similar questions for an employer or project manager who is supervising an employee who is undermining the culture of the company by their words, attitudes, and actions. No doubt there are lots of scenarios for these kinds of challenges and questions.

As parents, leaders, teachers, employers, and those who are responsible for a team, we need to set and maintain the values and culture for our families and groups that we oversee. When a child, student, or employee goes rogue, we need to have conversations to help that person think about their choices and consider the opportunity to do some recalibration.

As this relates to our families and having adult children, I've met more than a few Christian parents who have wrestled with their internal struggles over their children's choices. When the kids make choices that don't conform or reflect the ideals or the upbringing parents gave their children, or when children's values are drastically different from the values of the parents, they can cause hurt or disappointment.

There can be lots of angst and struggle when a child decides to live with their boyfriend of girlfriend before getting married. It can absolutely be a struggle when a child affirms a sexuality that isn't aligned with a biblical perspective, when they choose to enjoy alcohol when there was never booze in the house, etc. Thankfully, our Heavenly Father is well-versed in parenting children who don't always conform to His values. Indeed, I believe that our Heavenly Father prioritizes our hearts and relationship with Him over our achievements and piety, religious conformity, or our failures and immorality.

With these issues in mind, let's look at the father and his older son in our parable. I'd suggest that the dialogue between the father and his older son is reflective of what our Heavenly Father might say to us if our values and subsequent choices were to go rogue from His values. This is the core heartbeat of the parable—the father's values that are demonstrated with his sons.

In this parable, the older son learns about the welcome-home party for his brother and chooses to stay in the field, distancing himself from his dad and home. But what about the father? What does a parent do when a son or daughter gives a parent the stiff-arm treatment, pulling away and refusing to engage? This can be hurtful beyond words to a parent. The last thing in the world that we want to experience is distance or disconnect from our kids. But that's exactly what happens in this parable when the older son refuses to join the welcome party for his little brother. So what does the dad do?

Consider these various translations for the older son's reaction and the father's engagement for Luke 15:28:

*The older brother was angry and wouldn't go in. **His father came out and begged him*** (NLT).

*The older brother stomped off in an angry sulk and refused to join in. **His father came out and tried to talk to him**, but he wouldn't listen* (MSG).

> *The older son became angry and refused to go in and celebrate. So **his father came out and pleaded with him,** "Come and enjoy the feast with us!"* (TPT)

Culture and History

When we think about the fathers' actions, we also need to consider the history and culture in which this story is told. In this culture, a father wouldn't leave a party at his home to try to reconcile with his older, pouty son. It would be considered humiliating for a father to make this effort. The father was the head of the family, and everyone would customarily accommodate and respond to his leadership and align with his decisions. After all, he is the *pater familias*.

Nevertheless, just like he did for his younger son, the father goes out to try to reconcile with his older son, demonstrating again his value for connecting with his kids. On top of that, the father pleads with his oldest son, begging him to join the party. As we've already discussed, the older son presents his righteous indignation and justified anger.

When I read the conversation between the older son and his father at the end of the Prodigal Son parable, it's very disturbing to me for a variety of reasons. Maybe what is most unsettling is that we don't read about any reconciliation between this son and the father, even though this is one of the father's essential values. The oldest son expresses his hostility and resentment along with his feelings of being slighted and unappreciated by the extravagant welcome for his reprobate little brother. Jesus doesn't conclude the exchange with a "happily ever after" ending.

Jesus doesn't conclude the exchange with a "happily ever after" ending.

Nonetheless, the father's actions and reply demonstrate again his core desire to have a reconciled and connected relationship with his son, regardless of the choices his son makes. The challenge, however, is that his son's perspective is drastically different from his father's point of view. Maybe even more to the point, the son's values are not in alignment with his father's values, which is another place for us to pause and reflect for some possible applications.

Fatherly Values

Consider what the father says to his offended, pouty, and rogue son. "*Son*, you are always with me and all that I have is yours." It's important to consider these relationship foundations and family values as we read the father's reply to his son's anger. To begin, he addresses his son as "Son." This is noteworthy because it's a contrast to how his son begins this conversation. As we considered before, the older son replies with a "Look what I've done for you" attitude.

Additionally, the father tells this son, "You are always with me." Obviously, this isn't true because there are times they're apart, like when the welcome-home celebration was happening. Nevertheless, from the father's point of view and his core values, his older son is always with him. I think that the father is expressing how he wants things to be. He considers that his older son is always by his side. This would be another value that the father is contrasting with his son's choices. From the father's point of view, everything that he has belongs to his older son, while the older son complains about not having a young goat to celebrate with his friends. There's a significant chasm between the father's values and the perspective of his older son.

Let's consider how the father is responding to his oldest son, both in action and word. Here are some contrasts:

Oldest Son	Father
Refuses to go home	Comes out to his son
"Look!"	"Son"
I have been serving you and keeping your commandments.	You are always with me.
You never gave me a young goat to celebrate with my friends.	All that I have is yours.
Your loser son comes home and you throw him a party.	We have to celebrate and rejoice because your brother is home.

There's a drastic contrast between the values of the father and his older son's actions. The family values aren't remotely cohesive! The father speaks from his perspective of relationship, connection, family, generosity, and acceptance because those are his fundamental values and motives. Everything he does and says throughout the entirety of the parable is rooted in these values and motives. His words and actions with his older son reveal the vast differences between his values and the older son's choices and perspective.

The last sentence of the story is from the father to his elder son about the reprobate and now reconciled son / brother. We read, "But we had to celebrate and rejoice, for this brother of yours was dead and has begun to live, and was lost and has been found."

Celebration and Audience

Let's remember that Jesus is telling this parable to two main groups within His audience: tax collectors and sinners; Pharisees and scribes (the pious and upstanding law keepers). Reflect on the last sentence of the parable; Jesus is telling both audiences that the essential value and motive of our Father is that His children would be reconciled to Him, regardless of their piety or debauchery. The religious and pious leaders who were listening to Jesus would likely know that they're represented in this parable by the older son. At the same time, the parable father is reflecting the Heavenly Father, expressing the divine values of reconciliation, fatherhood, family, and so much more.

> *The essential value and motive of our Father is that His children would be reconciled to Him, regardless of their piety or debauchery.*

Why would we choose to live in the identity of a reprobate or righteous child of God when both identities could create isolation and exclusion from our Father's love for us? Let's allow ourselves to be wholly convinced that our Heavenly Father loves us, has compassion for us, and wants us to live in celebrated reconciliation with Him, regardless of our choices or mistakes! Let's remember that our Heavenly Father says over each of us, "For this child of mine was dead and has come to life again; he was lost and has been found."

CHAPTER SEVEN:
THE FATHER'S WANTS AND FAMILY VALUES

R&R: Reflect and Respond

1. In thinking about the father leaving the party to talk with his angry son, what are your thoughts about that and how does it make you feel?

2. Jesus finishes this parable with the father repeating his joy about the younger son being found and alive. But there's no resolution with the older son. What do you think about that?

3. How do you think the father felt about his older son's compliance, dutiful attention, and how he honored the commands of his father?

4. What are some ways that you could be the father in this parable?

_____

_____

5. Consider 1 John 3:1 (NASB): "See how great a love the Father has bestowed on us, that we would be called children of God; and such we are." In what ways do you see yourself as the younger son? In what ways do you see yourself as the older son?

_____

_____

6. How could you see yourself as God's son or daughter, in the simplest construct without failures or earnings?

_____

_____

CHAPTER EIGHT

BE A CHILD

When you were growing up, did you go to your friends' houses to play? Did you go to their houses to have a meal? Did you notice any differences at your friend's house compared to your home?

When I was about eight years old, I went to my friend's house just a few doors down. It was later in the afternoon, and I popped in to play for a short time before dinner. When I walked in the door, several kids were sitting around the formal dining room table with some kind of game on the table, and my friend invited me to join. I grabbed a chair, sat down, and tried to figure out what they were playing.

There was a board and a teardrop, diamond-shaped pointer, and each kid was asking a question to the pointer and board. They then watched as the pointer moved to "answer" the question. I asked my friend, "What's this game?" She replied, "Isn't it so cool?! It tells you answers to questions. It's called a Ouija board!" I immediately freaked out and said that I had to go home. My parents had warned me about Ouija boards being demonic, so I was uber freaked!

To make things stranger, my friend's mom agreed to walk me home, and she was acting really weird. She was kind of stumbling as she walked, talking weirdly, slurring her words, and being lots more friendly and cordial with me than she normally was with me. She walked me to my front door, rang the doorbell, and waited for someone to open the door. My mom opened the door and there was a brief exchange between them, relatively pleasant, before I zipped in the door.

Later, I talked with my mom about the experience, and she explained that the board they were playing with was indeed a Ouija board. Additionally, she explained that my friend's mom was acting weird because she was drunk. Both of these things, booze and Ouija boards, weren't in our home because the values of my parents didn't allow for them.

It's important to think about the values and experiences you received from your family. These things have a big impact on our worldview and how we view ourselves. These values show up in our choices and priorities and in our conversations and relationships. Sometimes we perpetuate the values we had in our childhood, while sometimes we are viscerally opposed to those values.

Sometimes we perpetuate the values we had in our childhood, while sometimes we are viscerally opposed to those values.

One of the essential values and goals of the Prodigal Son / Chasing Father parable is reconciling each son to his father. We see the father's passion bleeding through his embrace with his younger son and conversation with the older son. The father, representing our Heavenly Father, wants each son to live in reconciled communion with Himself, one of His most observable values.

Let's again remind ourselves that Jesus is telling this parable to two audiences: the sinners and the righteous. So ultimately, what Jesus is expressing through the parable is that the Heavenly Father wants His sinner children to be reconciled to Himself. The Heavenly Father wants His righteous children to be reconciled to Himself. Furthermore, it's not enough to pay lip service to being the father's son or daughter. It's not enough to just give a head nod to acknowledge a familial position.

The father in the parable wants his sons to live and be grounded in the reality of being his son, reflecting his values, living at home together, having fellowship and celebrations, and being wholly settled in the identity of sonship. As we absorb this, let's also acknowledge that Jesus is talking to us today about being the son / daughter of our Heavenly Father.

Maybe like me, you've often heard that you're God's daughter or son. But just because we hear things doesn't mean that we believe what we hear, nor do we have the values and internal framework to live as a fully loved, wholly celebrated, entirely welcomed son or daughter of God.

Indeed, I think that most of us behave from the values and identities that we received in our childhood. Some of those values were great, and others, not so much. Lots of the identities that we express today were formed in us from our childhood. I'd like to press into your awareness that it's possible that our values and identities might need to be more wholly calibrated to reflect the vibrant and expansive reality of living as God's son or daughter. To this end, let's consider some values we might have from our natural upbringing:

Being Frugal, Living in Scarcity

My dad grew up in the Depression era, a time when food was scarce, and it was really difficult to make money or have a job.

As a result, my dad was always looking for a bargain, buying dented cans of food at garage sales, and being overjoyed to get a significant discount on expired food. He saved everything and bought funky clothes, in part, because they were on sale. He passed along to me that we don't throw anything out, and eating possibly spoiled food is being frugal. He probably gave McDonald's the idea of having a dollar menu!

Orderly Home

In the Andrea family cameo, we read about her childhood home being totally messy and disheveled. Often, there were clothes strewn over all the furniture, shoe piles blocking doorways, and dirty dishes not only left in the sink but littering the kitchen counter. Growing up in such chaos had an intense impact on Andrea, such that she routinely maintains an orderly home. Of course, this can be a wonderful thing. But if this value isn't regulated, it can become a suffocating compulsion that drains away fun and relaxation to maintain a pristine and orderly home.

Rules Trump Relationship

In John's cameo, we read about his dad demanding quiet and etiquette at the dinner table and how this expectation created a tense experience for family dinners. As long as John did what his dad expected, dinner could be peaceful. Some of us grew up learning that we got attention and affection when we were good, when we achieved, and when we followed the rules. Others of us got attention by rebelling because even bad attention was better than no attention.

Performance Provides Value

Some of us grew up in a performance culture, such that we learned that second was the same thing as last. Nothing was acceptable if it wasn't first or best. Consequently, we are incredible achievers, and our accomplishments never seem to be satisfying or fulfilling because we are always aiming higher, striving to be even better, beyond the best. We find our value in what we do and accomplish, almost never in who we are—transactional living.

These are a few examples of values we might have from our upbringing. It is likely that many of our perceptions run opposite to being the wholly loved and fully treasured son or daughter of our Heavenly Father. Indeed, each son in the Prodigal Son parable didn't see himself as the valued and reconciled son of his dad. The younger son thought he'd lost his value and position as a son—unworthy. The older son served his dad and earned his position—more than worthy. But the father's heart toward each son was constantly working to reconcile his sons to live in their proper and accurate identity, not because of their actions, but because of his love.

This is also what our Heavenly Father wants for each of us. He doesn't want us to merely pay lip service to acknowledge being God's son or daughter. Instead, our Heavenly Father wants each of us to live in reconciled and accurate identity.

Our Heavenly Father wants each of us to live in reconciled and accurate identity.

Let's recall the basic viewpoints of each son in the parable as demonstrated in the interactions and communication with their dad. When the younger son returns home, he tells his dad that he's not worthy to be his son. Maybe you also have this point of view. You feel that you are not worthy, that you don't measure up, or that you've screwed up beyond redemption and you're lucky to be an outsider who gets crumbs and leftovers.

As for the older son, in his conversation with his dad, he reveals that he believes he is more than deserving and more than worthy because of his dutiful compliance and meticulous rigor to the rules and regulations. At the same time, he shows resentment, anger, pouting, and hostility toward his dad, as he feels slighted by the extravagant treatment his younger brother receives. The transactions aren't fair! The older son also compares himself to his brother and finds his brother lacking in his foolhardy and unrighteous behavior.

When I think about these two sons and who I identify with more, I have to say that I'm a little bit of each. In various seasons in my life, I'm more 80 percent older son and 20 percent younger son. At other times, I'm more like 75 percent younger son and 25 percent older son. But ultimately, I'm both sons, and I'm coming to understand that my Heavenly Father wants me to see myself the way that He sees me—as His beloved daughter with whom He wants to live in the reconciled reality. My Father wants me to know that I belong and I'm family because of who He is and His endless fatherly love for me. I know this to be true for you, as well, my beloved reader.

Love from our Heavenly Father can change the values and identities we received in our upbringing, helping us live in true alignment with our identity as God's son or daughter. Consider what John tells us: "See how great a love the Father has bestowed on us, that we would be called children of God; and such we are" (1 John 3:1 NASB). Because our upbringing was with earthly parents, we should let God work in our perceptions regarding our parents. We should let Him replace and adjust our perceptions so that they align with our Heavenly Father, from whom we have our true identity. Let's choose to live in the quality of our Father's love since we are His son or daughter.

Consider Jesus' conversation with Nicodemus in John 3, particularly at the beginning when He talks about being born of the flesh or born of the Spirit. Jesus says, "That which is born of the flesh is flesh, and that which is born of the Spirit is spirit" (John 3:6 NASB). I take this to mean that my flesh identity is grounded in being the daughter of Marilyn and Wallace Hickey; however, my core identity is grounded in being the daughter of God, rooted in genuine love and deeply treasured. While I love my earthly parents and I'm grateful for my upbringing, I'm coming to grow into a deeper connection with God as I increasingly recognize His design and identity in me. I've become keenly aware that Holy Spirit has an extremely central role to play in helping me stay grounded in my identity as God's daughter. I say this because of a few key verses.

The Spirit Himself testifies with our spirit that we are children of God (Romans 8:16 NASB).

Because you are sons, God has sent forth the Spirit of His Son into our hearts, crying, "Abba! Father!" (Galatians 4:6 NASB).

I've found these verses to be very helpful in lots of ways, particularly when I'm struggling with my identity, feeling insecure, stuck in a trauma rut, or messed up in my thinking. Indeed, these verses have become part of my daily routine to allow Holy Spirit to do alignment work in my identity. I still have wrestling matches and struggles in various seasons, conversations, and interactions, but I'm growing in my awareness of being God's daughter. Holy Spirit is helping that awareness to be more consistent and not as superficial as in my past.

In addition to growing in my awareness of being God's daughter, I'm also being challenged to recalibrate my values to better reflect my Heavenly Father's values. This is important and a fundamental shift in how I see the world, making adjustments to the values I acquired in my upbringing and moving more fully into my Father's values.

Earlier in the chapter, I talked about some identities and values that we might have acquired from our earthly parents. Some of these could include: living in scarcity, compulsive order in the home, rules trumping relationship, and performance making value. These are human values that don't fully align with our Father's values, although they have pieces and parts that are really great.

In terms of our Father's values, let's lived anchored in who the Father is as expressed in the Prodigal Son parable. This father did everything in his power to reconcile his sons from his heart overflowing with love. The father's love wasn't based on the actions of his sons, but rather on who the father was. Thinking about this can take away the transactional nature we often fall into with our Father: when I'm good, God loves me; when I'm bad, God doesn't love me as much. Do you really have so much power as to control or influence God loving you? Let's live in the truth that God loves us because that's who God is and not because of our piety, righteous choices, religious compliance, or upstanding voting record. Additionally, we didn't lose our Father's love because we ran away from His principles or directives.

The father's love wasn't based on the actions of his sons, but rather on who the father was.

Finally, in the parable, the father does everything in his power to reconcile each of his sons to himself, to their home and community. I'm challenged to let my Father's values overrun my criticism of other people, my judgment of their choices, my superior perspective about how I'm better than others, and my earned position in God's family because of my devout rigor and alignment with righteous living. I'm also challenged to let my Father's value for reconciliation exceed my failures, poor decisions, and reckless living.

I find myself in both the older and younger son in this parable, and I'm indescribably grateful that my Father loves me beyond my failures and righteous indignation. I'm aware that my Father wants me not only to live in His love but to also reflect His love and desire to reconcile to the people in my world.

Would you join me in this journey? This book is titled *The Road Home*, and it's all about coming home to our Father. Perhaps our Father would like not only to celebrate our return and identity as sons and daughters, but also to celebrate the people around us who are deeply loved and treasured as our Father's sons and daughters.

Welcome Home!

Let's roll out the welcome mat for all our Father's sons and daughters!

CHAPTER EIGHT:
BE A CHILD

R&R: Reflect and Respond

1. What are three values you received from your upbringing? Describe an event with each value that crystalized this in your childhood.

_____

_____

2. What are the strengths of these three values? What are the weaknesses in these values?

_____

_____

3. How do you feel and what do you think when you reflect on being the treasured son or daughter of your Heavenly Father?

_____

_____

4. What perceptions might you have that disagree with your Father's intense passion to reconcile? In what are your perceptions rooted? How did you acquire these perceptions?

_____

_____

5. Consider memorizing the following verses and integrating them into your daily living by including one or some of them as the home screen on your phone, sticky notes on your bathroom mirror, daily reminders put into your calendar, consistently praying a verse with a friend or with your kids, circling back to these questions in three months to reflect on possible changes.

> But as many as received Him, to them He gave the right to become children of God, even to those who believe in His name, who were born, not of blood nor of the will of the flesh nor of the will of man, but of God (John 1:12-13 NASB).

> That which is born of the flesh is flesh, and that which is born of the Spirit is spirit (John 3:6 NASB).

> For all who are being led by the Spirit of God, these are sons of God (Romans 8:14 NASB).

> The Spirit Himself testifies with our spirit that we are children of God (Romans 8:16 NASB).

> For you are all sons of God through faith in Christ Jesus (Galatians 3:26 NASB).

Because you are sons, God has sent forth the Spirit of His Son into our hearts, crying, "Abba! Father!" (Galatians 4:6 NASB)

See how great a love the Father has bestowed on us, that we would be called children of God; and such we are (1 John 3:1 NASB).

INTERMISSION

Now that you've finished the first part of this book, exploring the Prodigal Son parable as it's told in the Bible, I'm very eager for you to experience the Prodigal Son parable in a modern context. Having read the first part, you have been able to gain a deeper insight into Jesus' purposes and heart within this parable. Indeed, this parable lays the foundation for God as our Heavenly Father and our identity as God's son or daughter. This is essential for our existence, such that we appreciate that our identity isn't only grounded in our earthly upbringing or family.

In the second part of this book, you will read a modern allegory of this parable. You'll note in this modern rendition some very pivotal characters, just like Jesus' telling of the Prodigal story. It's also important to know that many of the characters in this allegory are the same characters from the allegory in the first book that Isabell and I wrote, *The Road to Wholeness*. This book revolves around Jesus' parable about the Good Samaritan, and it helps readers to recognize and deal with trauma to participate in God's healing and redemptive work throughout our lives.

Furthermore, since this allegory is set in our present world and a follow-up to Isabell's portion in *The Road to Wholeness*, there are some very intense scenes, conversations, and descriptions. Please note that it's possible that you might be disturbed or triggered by some of the modern retelling of the Prodigal Son. You might also find it helpful, if you haven't already, to read our book on trauma, appreciating that God's designs and purposes in our lives include healing, redemption, and reconciling us to Him as our loving Heavenly Father.

> *God's designs and purposes in our lives include healing, redemption, and reconciling us to Him as our loving Heavenly Father.*

With that said, the story that you're about to read will speak to our Father's deep passion to reconcile each of us into His family. To this end, we hope that you can see at least part of yourself in each of the characters in the parable of the Prodigal's Son.

I'm super proud of my daughter, Isabell! She's written this allegory for you to connect in our modern living to Jesus' timeless parable. It's our honor to co-author this book for not only your pleasure, but also your spiritual growth. We want you to live more wholly reconciled with your Heavenly Father, in your true home and family with God!

Warning: some scenes, language and content in this allegory have the potential to trigger or evoke strong emotions in a reader, possibly stirring up memories that have been hurtful. It is our prayer that you will experience the reconciling and redemptive work of the Holy Spirit in your soul, to transform your awareness to the reality of being God's beloved son or daughter.

Let's jump into our modern allegory to the Prodigal's Son and experience our Father's loving posture and journey to redeem us wholly into His family!

MODERN ALLEGORY FOR THE PRODIGAL SON

What you are about to read is a story. In the scriptures, Jesus told His followers stories to help them understand complicated theological ideas, and those who had ears to hear, heard the stories and learned the lessons. In the same way, I have attempted to rewrite one of His parables into modern times. The savvy reader will recognize the references to *Road to Wholeness*, but for argument's sake, let me remind you where we left off.

When last we spoke, the small town of Smythville had been ravaged by a vigilante gang called the POTG, the Punishers of the Guilty. This vigilante gang was run by a horrible man named Jupiter, and his girlfriend, Savannah, was his right-hand woman. The gang had attacked one innocent man, Jerome Gorinski, whose life was saved by a Good Samaritan and a local innkeeper named Lydia.

Due to the complicated, and human, aspects addressed in this story, there are references to drug and alcohol abuse and addiction, domestic violence and sexual assault, and a variety of traumatic events. It is my hope and prayer that while you read this story, the Lord is able to do a work of grace and healing in your heart, and also in your families.

CHAPTER 1

TRAGEDY

When Lydia Gresham first lay her eyes on her oldest daughter, she fell head over heels in love. This perfect bundle of joy nestled herself into Lydia's heart and stayed there. She had waited for her miracle for the last twenty years, and every second of the waiting had been worth it. She had been working as a nurse, and had watched women go through pregnancy, loss, birth, all stages of life. Every time she helped a mother, there was a tug on her heart, and she would beg, plead the Lord to send her a child. Finally, He did and her sweet Mary was the answer to all her prayers.

Her doctors had been pessimistic about a woman in her late forties having one child, let alone two, but two years and countless prayers later, Lydia found herself pregnant again and panicking. Would she be able to love this second child as much as little Mary? She spent her nights sitting in the rocking chair in the new nursery, eating pretzels and crying, before her husband inevitably put her back to bed, leaving the pretzels behind.

When her second daughter arrived, kicking and screaming, Lydia discovered that she was indeed capable of loving her as much. Her second daughter, who her husband insisted be named after his grandmother Savannah, joined her sister in Lydia's heart. As she lay in bed watching her sleep, she made her daughter a promise.

"Never," she said, "I will never let you feel second in anything."

The years went by, and as her daughters grew from babies to children to teenagers, one of her greatest joys was learning who they were as individuals. Mary, her oldest, took after her, softer from the onset, but with a scary determination when she came under pressure. One year, Mary entered the science fair, determined to beat her rival Billy Cohan. Lydia and her husband had privately laughed when Mary told them that she was going to win. What a silly thing to say! She had never showed even a modicum of interest in science.

But Mary went with her mother to work every Saturday for a month, learning about all things medicine and what it meant to be a nurse. When the time came for her to present her project, she gave a flu shot to an orange, presented the history of vaccinations, and shared how a vaccine's dead virus creates white blood cells and antibodies to defeat the flu virus. Billy Cohan made a paper mâché volcano. She won by a landslide.

On the other hand, her younger daughter, Savannah, was like her father. She had an ability to feel every emotion at its largest possible volume. From meltdowns in grocery stores to tear-filled renditions of her favorite love songs screamed out the windows of the family van, Lydia was often overwhelmed by her youngest daughter's emotional outbursts.

Her husband, however, who had his own journey with navigating emotions, came to her rescue every time. He wiped away her tears, hugged away the pains of a fall, and collapsed laughing from the smallest joke. As she learned and grew, Lydia received instincts of steel when it came to her daughters. She knew when to ground them, when to listen, when to cook, and when to go out to eat. Together, she and her husband tried to overcome every single problem and give their daughters the love and support that they both needed. At night, they dreamed about the hotel they would open when they retired, planning everything from the decorations to the food they would serve for breakfast. In those days, every dream seemed reachable. They would pray over their family, over their dreams, and Lydia felt that they could do anything, with each other and the Holy Spirit.

The girls fought, like any sisters would, but their fights were short-lived and quickly resolved. Mary's fear of disappointing her parents always led her to apologize first, and Savannah's impulsive emotions lead to tear-filled apology hugs, more often than not. Her two daughters were friends, pals, and they stuck by each other.

Then, the girls entered high school. When Mary started, Lydia was thrilled that her oldest daughter showed a penchant for nursing. She fostered this love in her daughter, encouraged difficult classes, and offered ideas about working for a clinic after school. She had to keep herself from pushing too hard. Mary excelled at everything, and Lydia had to remind herself that she was still a little girl, not a grown-up yet.

Savannah followed her sister in high school two years later, and suddenly Lydia found herself playing defense. She fought every single boyfriend, spent hundreds of dollars on hobbies that Savannah dropped within a month, and endured screaming matches that left her with a headache and a weepy heart. Her one respite was that she and her husband grew closer every day. They held each other back from pushing Mary to her break-ing point, worried together when Savannah didn't come home, doled out punishments and rewards, and joined ranks when the girls tried to secretly adopt a puppy.

Life was difficult, but she began to love this new season in their family. She loved watching her daughters hang on to things from their childhood and learn new words and mannerisms. She began to glimpse what kind of woman each of her girls were becoming. Through it all, she fell deeper and deeper in love. Every year, she fell more in love with her daughters, her husband, and even herself. The current of love that ran through her family led her deeper and deeper into the Lord's heart. These felt like the best days of her life.

Lydia woke up one Monday afternoon with a pit in her stomach. The girls were at school, and she had worked the night shift. The clock read 2 p.m. She had a hard time figuring out whether this was her normal exhaustion or something else.

No, something was very, very, *very* wrong.

She sat on her bed and stared at the phone until it finally rang. It was an unknown number. She took a deep breath and waited, clinging to her last moment of ignorance for as long as possible.

"Hello," she finally whispered into her cellphone.

"Mrs. Gresham, there's been a terrible accident."

She was quiet. It couldn't be her girls, it just couldn't.

"I'm afraid your husband was in a car accident and...ma'am we're going to need you to come to the hospital."

Lydia felt like she was dreaming, as she grabbed her keys, and drove the familiar route to the hospital. She saw a police car outside and parked behind it, her urgency only growing.

"Mrs. Gresham, please follow me," said the officer, leading her in. They rushed to a trauma room, where the doctor stood outside shaking his head.

"Lydia," he said, recognizing her. "I'm so sorry. We did everything we could, but...he died while we were trying to resuscitate him."

Lydia gave a sob and sank to the ground. He was gone. Her husband, her best friend, was gone. What was she going to do?

In the weeks that followed, it seemed to Lydia that her home had collapsed. The girls spent all their time in the house, and the three of them moved around as if in a daze. Savannah spent each night falling asleep on one of the couches in the living room, and Mary joined her when she was feeling lonely and sad. Lydia took time off of work and spent her days in bed. She couldn't get out of bed most days, and felt herself slipping.

One night, the two girls crawled into bed with her, and the three of them just lay there, crying and hugging. Lydia woke up with Savannah snuggled under her chin and Mary sleeping on her other side.

They need me, she thought. She got out of bed, wrote a note to her daughters, and drove to work. She worked a quick shift, just to get back in the swing of things, and when she returned the girls were watching TV together. She grabbed the remote and turned off the screen, forcing them to look at her.

"Tonight, we are going out to eat. Tomorrow, we will go back to school and work."

The girls looked wary, but Lydia insisted.

They all took showers and got ready. For Lydia, this was her first shower since her husband died, and seeing his shampoo brought her to tears all over again. But, by the time she was presentable, the girls looked rested. The three of them walked down to the diner a few blocks from their house.

"Mom," Mary asked, keeping her eyes on the pavement ahead of her, "what's going to happen to us?"

"Honey, I don't know. Right now, we're going to eat our weight in French fries and ice cream, but I know that we're going to be okay, no matter what happens."

"Do you promise?" whispered Savannah, tears coming to her eyes.

Lydia put her arm around Savannah's shoulders and kissed her forehead. "I promise."

The diner was on Main Street. The place was packed on a Friday night, and as the three of them walked in, silence fell for half a beat too long before the three of them were hustled into a booth. The sticky air smelled of fried food and lemon cleaner, and Lydia immediately felt settled into the familiarity of it.

Elizabeth, their favorite waitress, brought over sodas for the girls and coffee for Lydia. She leaned on the booth and exchanged pleasantries, complimenting the girls and winking at them. A massive basket of fries arrived and when Lydia looked around, her neighbors raised their drinks to her in a silent salute. The girls were distracted by the fries, but Lydia held her coffee cup up and smiled.

She felt the tension in the diner ease as people came up to say hello. Savannah's school friend came over to ask if she wanted to walk to school with her tomorrow, and Mary's favorite science teacher gave her a big, long hug. Elizabeth steered them all away and brought out sandwiches.

"Thank you," Mary said, and Savannah gave Elizabeth a sheepish look over her grilled cheese. As they ate, Lydia began to talk about their dad for the first time since he died.

"He was the best man I ever knew," she said, pausing to chew her Reuben.

Mary smiled at her and raised her milkshake in a toast. "To dad."

"To dad," they echoed and clinked their glasses.

Later that night, they got ready for school the next day. Mary rifled through her notebooks, triple-checking that everything was packed, and Savannah tried on so many outfits that her room turned into a clothing tornado.

Lydia began to feel slightly panicked. Mary was so detail-oriented, and Savannah so impulsive. How could she navigate her two prides and joys alone?

She felt the Holy Spirit draw close to her heart, soothing her fears into calm and comforting her.

I am with you. Prepare your heart.

CHAPTER 2

SQUANDERING

Savannah sat on the side of the road, mindlessly scrolling through her phone. The hum of an engine grabbed her attention and she automatically smiled as she saw Jupiter coasting his bike.

"Hey, babe," he said, tucking her hair behind her ear and leaning out for a kiss. She obliged, slinging her gym bag across her shoulders as she hopped on behind him. She and Jupiter had been living together for a couple of months now, and she was so happy.

Her sparring partner left the gym, waving at her on his way out, and she waved back. Jupiter tensed his body in front of her, and she knew that a conversation would follow. He hated that her Krav Maga partners were all guys, but there was nothing she could do about it. Girls didn't really go to her martial arts gym, and she needed to practice.

After her dad died, Savannah had a hard time making peace with the world around her. The gym was the one place where she could let out her anger, frustration, and pain, and no one got hurt. She remembered the first time she saw Jupiter in the gym. He was punching the bag in the corner, and she was mesmerized, watching him move. When he finally looked up and caught her staring at him, she blushed, and went back to her reps. He walked up to her, introduced himself, and the rest was history. She moved out of her mom's house soon after, and their life together had begun.

Savannah sighed, not wanting to have another conversation about her choice of gym and sparring partner. Maybe she could buy his buddies pizza to make it up to him. Her dread grew as she thought about the group of guys waiting at their apartment. Jupiter had a magnetic personality, and she knew that these hangers-on were a necessary evil.

She felt a pang of guilt as they passed the diner on Main Street, remembering her sister and mom, but it was drowned by a laugh as Jupiter revved the engine on the way out of town. He jumped the bike, and she shrieked, holding him tighter and laughing harder.

As they neared their apartment complex, she rested her head on his back and matched her breathing to his. For now, it was the two of them. The idea of forever kept her going for months, but lately she was having fleeting ideas that it would never be the two of them again. She swallowed, already tasting the beer waiting for her.

Savannah opened the door and immediately tripped over a pair of size 13 sneakers. The guys in the living room laughed as she picked herself up. Face flaming, she glared around, trying to find the owner of the shoes.

"Shut up!" Jupiter snapped from the kitchen, and silence fell immediately. Marcus, one of his childhood friends, smirked at her and took a drag from his cigarette, daring her to say something. Savannah rolled her eyes and went into the kitchen for her beer. Jupiter kissed her, whispering apologies, and so she smiled and grabbed her beer, kissing him back and pulling her long, blonde hair up into a ponytail.

She and Jupiter moved to the living room couch, where she nestled into him, taking a long drink and preparing for the next event. It was time for Jupiter's favorite pastime: watching the news.

They'd been following the story of Bill, a man who assaulted his wife. Their town jail was constantly being filled and emptied, but Bill had been arrested multiple times. This time, his wife was not backing down. She wanted justice.

Savannah was obsessed with Maria, the wife, whom she had seen at a grocery store with a huge bruise on her chin. That night, she saw Maria on the news and looked into the eyes of the man who had hit her. Savannah cried, and Jupiter held her, assuring her that Bill would get what was coming to him.

Tonight, they watched the news report as the jury voted not guilty, and Savannah's heart dropped.

"What?" she whispered breathlessly. The picture cut to a live feed of Bill outside the courthouse, smirking and waving at the crowd gathered. The doorbell rang, and one of the guys got up to grab the pizzas, startling her out of her daze. She grabbed another beer for Jupiter and a water bottle for herself, before she saw that Jupiter wasn't eating.

"You know what?" he asked, standing up, and pushing the beer away, "I think this garbage town and its police are going down." The whole group fell silent as he continued to trash the police and threaten the man on the TV screen.

Everyone was at least two drinks in when Jupiter brought up the idea of hunting Bill down. Savannah's sadness had long since turned to anger, and she cheered with the rest of them, climbing into the van and blasting music. The van belonged to Marcus, Jupiter's best friend, but Jupiter drove. Marcus stumbled into the van, slurring his words and Savannah shook her head, laughing, as she slid into the front seat.

They found Bill walking his dog. Savannah almost felt bad. Here was a man who was already taking care of his animal, hours after being released from jail. Maybe he was a changed man, like he claimed in his defense. She remembered the bruise on Mary's face, and her doubts died before she voiced them.

Bill walked up to his door, and his wife brought him a bottle, smiling hesitantly. From the van on the opposite side of the street, the group watched him read the label. It was like everything went in slow motion. Savannah only had time to scream "No!" before she saw him throw the bottle down and slap Maria across the cheek. Jupiter turned to her, a new look in his eyes.

"What do we do, babe?"

She smiled, savoring the feeling of justice. "Let's punish him."

Later that night, after they had beat Bill within an inch of his life, the group was riding a high, literally. They opened up the expensive booze, Savannah took hits from a joint, and Jupiter got very drunk.

"You know what?" he yelled, standing up, and raising the bottle of liquor high.

"What?" they all yelled. Savannah giggled and watched him command the room.

"We're the only ones who care about these people!" Jupiter said, taking another drink from the amber bottle. "Let's make this official!"

Savannah thought for a second that he was talking to her, and she felt a pinch of panic, before she realized he was talking about starting a group. The weed made her slow, and agreeable, and she found herself cheering. Was she supposed to be suspicious of something?

"Are you with me?" he asked, grabbing her by the face and looking right in her eyes. Through the haze, she realized this was an important moment, so she sobered up as much as she could.

"Until I die," she said. He grinned and kissed her deeply. The group around her cheered when she laughed and kissed him back. This was the best moment of her life, or so she thought.

That night, the weight of what they had done settled in and while Jupiter slept, she slunk quietly into the bathroom, softly closing the door and turning on the lights. She turned on the sink and splashed water on her face, staring at her reflection. She raked her hands through her hair, letting out a shaky breath. A scared, lonely girl looked back at her. She remembered Bill's scream of pain, and she retched over the toilet, throwing up all the liquor in her stomach. When she was done, she splashed some water on her face and went back to bed. Jupiter was awake and he held his hand out to grab hers.

"He deserved it," he said, softly, but firmly.

"I know," she whispered back, taking his hand and sitting on the edge of the bed.

"Think about his wife. How much danger she was in. Something needed to be done. She is safe now, because of us, because of you!" he said, stroking her hair.

Savannah hadn't thought of that. He was right. She smiled up at him, gave him a quick kiss, and turned back to go to sleep, confident that they had done the right thing.

The group started to keep track of the people around town who they wanted to punish. Savannah worked a remote job, so it gave her enough time to dig through social media accounts and new reports. But that wasn't enough for Jupiter.

A few months later, he asked her to quit her job and become his researcher. She was in charge of selecting the guilty ones to punish. Whenever she found one, he was the one to plan the punishments. They were a perfect team. He was always complimenting her, and she savored his praise. The more that Jupiter's club, the Punishers Of The Guilty, did for the community, the more ruthless and distant he got, which pushed Savannah to work even harder. The punishments were violent and terrifying, and he started using her Krav Maga training. He wanted her to beat the guilty victims, and she was happy to oblige, for him. She did it all for him, every blow that landed, every slash that drew blood, she always looked to Jupiter, and he was always smiling.

She had originally trained to learn self-defense. The novelty of the club wore off, and soon she started drinking all the time. The alcohol helped dull her senses and hone in on her one goal: to make Jupiter happy and proud.

When he first approached her and asked her to start learning new fighting techniques, she agreed, but was secretly hesitant. Savannah didn't enjoy the punishments like he did. She still couldn't punish anyone sober. But, as time went on, Jupiter drank less, smoked less, and spent more time on the internet campaigning for members and pushing the group to be their best. She wanted to be the best she could, for him. So, one day at the gym, she picked up a police baton.

"Hit it," Jupiter said, holding the punching bag. She hit the bag with a satisfying *thunk* and thought of Maria, the woman whose husband they punished. Her bruised face appeared in her mind, and she started hitting the bag harder and harder.

"Good job," Jupiter said, giving her an appreciative nod before moving on to another member of the club. She began to train harder and harder. During the day, she trained and researched, and at night they stalked their next guilty man or woman before finally executing the punishment.

One day, a strange man showed up at their apartment door, asking for Jupiter. He wore a black fedora and had thick eyeliner, more than Savannah ever wore. He had a permanent smirk, and refused to look her in the eyes.

"Matthew!" Jupiter said, walking to the door. He smiled and clapped the new man on the back. Savannah nervously fidgeted with her hair, wrapping the strands around her fingers.

"Did you bring the goods?" Jupiter asked. Matthew's smirk deepened into a smile as he opened his bag, showing him a group of evil-looking knives. Jupiter rubbed his hands together excitedly, and ushered him inside.

She did not go with them to the punishment that night, but Jupiter showed her pictures, pausing at each one to explain what happened. Their latest victim had a taste for flirting with young girls, and when Jupiter shared his story on the online forum, a man had offered his services. As she watched him scroll through the photos, Savannah pasted on a smile, but when he finally fell asleep, she ran into the kitchen and took a long swig from a bottle of vodka. It was too much and that was only the beginning. Soon, more and more guys from out of town were showing up on her doorstep, all with a vendetta and a plan. They came from Jupiter's online forums, which he mercilessly ruled over. To Savannah, it seemed like everything was changing, so much.

Watching the news was one thing that stayed consistent. The more that national news developed the story about their club, the happier Jupiter was. His punishments got flashier, and Savannah took to drinking all day. She wanted to do whatever he asked, but when she slept, sometimes she had nightmares about the people they punished. Whenever she woke up screaming, Jupiter held her, reminding her that the targets were guilty and dirty, and reminding her of all the victims of assault and other crimes they were saving. She fell asleep in his arms more often than not. He whispered plans to her. Plans of big houses, fast cars, clean streets for their children. His voice soothed her into dreamless sleep.

Savannah was unloading the groceries with another girlfriend of a visiting "punisher" when her phone dinged. She looked down and paused when she saw her mother's face. After all this time, her mother still texted once a month to check up on her, and it never stopped freaking her out. Her hair was falling out of the clip, and she reached up to fasten it tighter. Now was not the time.

She shook off the memories of her mom and put another case of beer in the fridge, taking one out for herself. They had another guy to punish tonight. She had been watching him online for weeks. He was cheating on his wife, and Jupiter did not like cheaters. This one was going to be ugly, and she needed liquid courage.

The punishment did not go well.

Jupiter was furious. After they got back to the apartment, he had jumped on his motorcycle and disappeared. Savannah hadn't seen him in hours. The POTG club had basically moved in, so she spent all her time in her and Jupiter's bedroom. But tonight, she sat on the stairs outside of the apartment, nursing a cigarette next to Marcus.

"What a wimp," Marcus said, tapping his own cigarette. Savannah didn't say anything. Jupiter's newest guest had vomited on the guilty man, and Jupiter had lost it. He had pulled a knife on the guest, demanding that he scrub the body and the scene of all his DNA. The rest of them had stood by as the guest did just that, shame and guilt evident. Savannah had never gotten sick again at a punishment, and Jupiter never brought up the first night.

The rev of the engine startled them both, and she snubbed out the cigarette, standing to meet him. When Jupiter walked up, she wrapped her arms around him, but he pulled back, glaring at her.

"What's going on here?" he asked, shifting his glare to Marcus.

"Nothing," Marcus said. "We were just waiting for you."

Jupiter shot him another glare and pulled a long, blonde hair from Marcus's shoulder. His t-shirt must have snagged it when he sat down next to her, but Jupiter's glare had turned lethal. She panicked and grabbed his hand. "Let's go," she said, all but dragging him into the apartment.

The next morning, Marcus didn't show up for breakfast, but when he finally walked in, he had news.

"Bro, remember that reporter chick who used to live in town? She's back! I heard her asking Elizabeth about the club at the diner."

Jupiter sat back, smiled, and said, "Let's give her something to report on."

The next few months were torture for Savannah and the guilty people in Smythville. To get the reporter's attention, Jupiter demanded that they punish one guilty person a week. That was too much for Savannah, but he required that she be at every punishment.

One day, she hadn't been able to find any guilty person, and he snapped.

"Get in the van," he yelled, and they all piled in. Savannah sat shotgun and watched him. He drove around town like a maniac, weaving through streets and alleyways.

"Let's find a nice homeless guy," one of the guys in the back said, laughing.

"No, let's find some idiots in an affair," another one countered.

"No. Let's get him," Jupiter said, pointing to a figure on the country road walking by himself. Savannah gulped, allowing the adrenaline of the moment to spur her as they pulled up. She recognized the MMA fighter, Jerome Gorinski, and Jupiter gave a laugh of pleasure, before putting the car in park. It was time to practice.

Later, Savannah shook as she washed the blood off of her hands in the shower. Jupiter had changed. She kept remembering his eyes as he drove away from the body, wild and crazy.

"Let's leave him," he said, as they peeled away from the body. "He's dead either way."

She shivered and watched the blood wash down the drain. Her hair had taken on a red hue, and she shampooed it three times, trying to wash the blood out. She finished her shower, put on a t-shirt, and got into bed, still shaking. She could hear Jupiter in the living room, cheering and drinking, so she fell asleep alone, afraid of what tomorrow would bring.

Sure enough over the next several days, Jupiter kept asking for more and more. The news spread that Jerome, the MMA fighter they beat up, had lived. The man, who they had beaten and left for dead, had survived. Jupiter was enraged, but luckily questions arose about the carving in his chest.

"Who is the POTG?" everyone seemed to ask. Jupiter decided to ride this wave, carving the initials or stapling notes to all their targets. On top of that, something had changed between the two of them. Their relationship had shifted. She tried avoiding him, but he was everywhere she went, at the grocery store, in their apartment, even on her walks outside of town, he was always there.

One day, Savannah walked into the gym, ready for a workout that would hopefully leave her gasping and perfectly exhausted. To her surprise, Jupiter was waiting for her.

"Come spar with me!" he said, wrapping his hand around her waist. She followed, confused.

"What about my class?" she asked, watching as her Krav Maga class started in the back studio.

"I thought today it could be just you and me," he said firmly.

Savannah paused. They had worked out together before, but this felt different. As they began to spar in the ring, she didn't see his playful, flirty smile. All she saw was him glaring at all the other guys in the gym. When she finally ended their session, she went to stretch, and he followed her.

"What are you doing?" she whispered as he stood behind her.

"Just making sure you're safe," he smiled at her and flicked her ponytail. "There's a lot of messed-up guys out there. You never know who you can trust."

Her heart sank into her toes as he continued to glare at other gym goers as she went through her stretches. Miles, her friend from high school, waved. She felt Jupiter's eyes on her as she ignored him and went into the next stretch.

Every day was like that. Jupiter never left her side, and soon she realized that he was using her phone a lot more. She was afraid, all the time. One night, Marcus bumped into her in the kitchen, and, faster than lightning, Jupiter pinned him against the counter with a knife to his throat.

"Don't touch what's mine," he said, winking at her. She smiled, but inside, her stomach turned. For the first time, she didn't feel safe around Jupiter, the man she loved. She wanted to throw up.

No. She wanted to get out. But how? She opened up her phone to text her mom almost every day, but Jupiter watched her text messages.

One night, she pretended that she was sick and stayed home from the punishment, drinking and crying. She had a drunken, crazy, perfect idea.

Before she chickened out, she pulled out her phone and googled *anonymous police tip*. She called the number and whispered into the phone.

"There's going to be a drug deal at the gym on Main Street tomorrow morning."

The POTG members all had a drug of choice, but Jupiter supplied them all. He had started buying weed from a guy at their gym, and Savannah went with him to get this week's supply. But the police were nowhere to be found. She shook her head. That's what she got for trusting the police in this town.

They took the bike home, and she realized that she had left her bracelet at the gym.

"Leave it," Jupiter said. "I'll buy you a hundred bracelets."

She shook her head so hard that it hurt. "My dad bought me that," she said, grabbing the keys from him and starting the engine. He moved to stand in front of the bike, crossing his hands over his chest, an amused look on his face.

"Fine," she snapped, yanking the keys out and throwing them at him. "I'll walk."

He was too shocked to follow, and she stormed toward the gym, pausing only when she heard sirens. She walked up and froze when she saw the owner of the studio and the local jeweler talking to a police officer. The jeweler pointed at her and the police pulled their guns out.

"On the ground!" they yelled, and she carefully lay down, too scared and tired to do anything but comply.

As they cuffed her, she began to panic. What was she going to do? In a moment of bravery, or perhaps stupidity, she saw the light at the end of the tunnel and screamed, "I know who runs the POTG club!"

CHAPTER 3

RESPONSIBILITY

Mary leaned back against the door. Another victim. Another note. Another case. She was seeing these people in her dreams, and they all pointed fingers at her, chanting, "Guilty! Guilty! Guilty!"

She had sent Julie Schafer, the reporter who was looking into the POTG club, down to Jerome's room. Thinking of Jerome reminded her, and she pulled out her phone to send her mother a text.

Mary: Jerome is doing well. He's in good spirits today.

Her mom responded within the minute.

Mom: Thank you my dear! Will you be home for dinner?

Mary: No, I'm working a double shift.

Mom: No worries. Love you!

"Code blue, code blue," echoed through the hallways, interrupting her text back. She darted out of the way as the crash team ran by her. She looked at her watch and yawned, stretching her neck and shaking her heard. The nurse's station had snacks and coffee, both of which she gratefully accepted.

Her charts were a mess. She started recording the vitals of her latest admit, a new victim of the POTG club. Mary's conversation with Julie lingered in her mind as she recorded numbers and observations. There were too many victims, each brutalized in ways that she could hardly comprehend. Of course, she had been aware of the club, but it was only a couple months ago that things got serious for her.

Thinking of her mother's story always brought a ball of anxiety up into her chest, and today was no different. Her mother was careful, calculating, and Mary had aspired to be like her every day of her life. It started when she won the science fair in grade school. The look of pride on her mother's face lit a fire inside of her that spurred Mary through high school, her father's death, nursing school, and her job. Everything she did was so that she could see that look of pride in her mom's eyes. But when Jerome, the victim of the POTG club, had arrived at her mom's motel that night, things changed. She still craved her mother's praise, but now she wanted her kept safe even more. This club had infiltrated her carefully planned life, and she had panicked. In nursing school, her friends and teachers had joked about how she was intensely and obsessively organized and proactive. She planned for every outcome, but she had never planned for the POTG, or for Jerome.

She put her head in her hands, remembering the phone call from her mom, how she calmly explained the situation to her and asked for her help. Mary had sprung into action, making calls and informing the ER that she would be subbing in. She had enough goodwill to snag a specialized assignment to Jerome's post-op care, and she kept a careful watch over him. When he told her what happened, her mind went blank.

How could someone do that? She had thought, and lost sleep for several nights mulling it over. The night he shared his story, she had stayed up all night, drinking cup after cup of tea, trying to calm her nerves. She checked her door locks at least twenty times.

That night, it was too much. She finally gave up on sleep and drove to her childhood home. Her mom had held her while she shook and shook and shook, unable to focus even for a second. She had moved in that night, and let her lease expire.

Her whole life, her mom had been her person. After her father died, she leaned into her mom even more. Mary wanted to step up and prove she could be like her. She watched her mom pull herself up from the darkest depression and bring their family into the light. So, when she saw her mother caring for others with the kind of care that demanded no return, she had made a vow to be the same. So every day she buckled down and worked. And the next day. And the next day.

Her mom never brought up the night she moved in, but she started checking in on her regularly. These daily texts only made Mary feel more guilty, so she started working harder at home, proving to her mom that she was fine. She worked more shifts, oversaw Jerome's care, and even became friends with Julie, the reporter who was writing a piece on the POTG club. She was bringing justice the only way she knew how, by helping shine light on the terrible things this club was doing.

Today, however, as she typed up the notes on her patient, she ran her tongue over her teeth, thinking. She didn't think anyone saw her talking to Julie. Even if they did, the nurses on this floor were like her family. They covered for each other, celebrated life moments, and saw each other through the darkest moments in each other's lives. That was why she was working a double shift. One of her friends had the nastiest flu she had ever seen. So she covered for her.

One of her patient's call buttons beeped, so she went back to work, leaving her fears behind. This patient had a broken hip, and Mary hated taking care of her. She reminded Mary of her mother. The woman was younger than her, but now Mary was seized with panic every time she saw her mother climbing a ladder or walking to the diner in the rain.

When she got back to the nurse's station, a new folder with an angry sticky note was waiting for her. Another new case. Mary rolled her eyes as her friends shot her sympathetic looks.

"What a nightmare," said Korban, another nurse and her best friend on the floor.

"Yeah," she agreed. "I already have that POTG guy. I don't think I can do another one."

Korban's face darkened, and Mary mentally kicked herself.

"I'll take him," he said quietly. Korban's sister had been another one of the victims. She handed over the file, giving his shoulder a squeeze as she went to fill up her water bottle.

Savannah may be gone, but that was much better than suffering. Mary hadn't seen her sister in years and had long since given up trying to find her. Savannah and Mary had always had a complicated relationship. After their father died, she had hoped that Savannah would help her out, maybe act like an adult. But Savannah was selfish, lonely, and wild. She and Mary fought even more, sometimes going for days without speaking. Savannah's constant tears confused her, and Mary didn't understand how someone could cry that much. One year, she came home for summer break and Savannah was nowhere to be found. Her mother didn't say anything, so she asked about her sister at dinner that night.

Her mother drew a very clear boundary.

"She's gone," her mother had said that night in the diner.

"Gone?" Mary asked, confused.

"She asked me for her college fund and moved out."

Mary took a drink of water to hide her scoff. "Where is she now?"

"I don't know."

Mary was furious. Her little sister had just left? "But—"

"Enough," her mother interrupted, gently but firmly. "Savannah is an adult and can make her own choices."

What is she thinking? Mary fumed that night, driving back to campus. *My sister is such a selfish little brat.*

She tried to bring her up every so often, but her mother had set a firm boundary—she would not talk about Savannah, and eventually Mary had given up. Savannah was a memory, but sometimes that memory was closer than usual. When she had cleaned the hotel after Jerome had been admitted, all Mary could think of was her sister. She was terrified that she could still be in town, still in danger. Every so often, she thought she saw Savannah on the back of a motorcycle, but every time she went to look closer, the bike had already sped off.

Mary missed her sister. She didn't miss the fights, or the tears, but she missed having her around. They had only had each other, and when she left, Mary had lost a piece of her home. She knew that Savannah had wanted a fresh start, but she felt abandoned, neglected. Sometimes, when she was particularly tired and angry, that missing feeling turned into anger. Mary was angry at her sister, which lead to guilt, which lead to more anger. It was a complicated process, and Mary didn't do complicated emotions. So she tried not to think about her.

Savannah's room in the house stayed empty, and her absence was felt, especially around their small town. People asked about her, but the Greshams had their answers so well practiced that it became second nature.

"She's gone."

After she began to take care of Jerome, Mary lived in fear all the time. She was petrified that the club would hear how her mother helped rescue their victim and target their family. So she took special care to keep her mom's identity a secret, even asking Jerome not to tell anyone. So, when Julie, the reporter, came looking for a hotel owner named Lydia, Mary wasn't too happy. Her mother had been caught up in this nightmare against her will, and she didn't want her mother to have to recount the whole horrible night again.

But her mother was selfless and kind. And Mary trusted Julie. So she listened to her mother's account of that night, again. No matter how many times she walked through it, Mary felt sick. The cruelty of the club was revolting, and she couldn't imagine the kind of people who could do that.

As she returned to her floor, the sound of a call button echoed through the halls, and Mary was caught up in the hustle of her floor, Savannah retreating to the back of her mind.

CHAPTER 4

CAME TO HERSELF

Savannah was tired. She had just told the reporter, Julie Scha-fer, everything, on the record, and she hoped that it would be enough to at least get some attention. The cop who took Julie's place kept talking, but she tuned him out, focusing on her breathing as she realized she hadn't had a drink in hours. She could feel a headache forming, and her hands started shaking.

"Can I please have a glass of water?" she asked. He brought her a plastic cup and she took a shaky drink.

"We need to know their names," he said, throwing away her empty cup. She pondered for a minute. The high of telling her story was falling away. All that was left was her in this cell with no plans, no friends, no family, nothing.

Well, she thought, *not nothing*. She thought about her mom, and their quiet, simple hotel, and suddenly everything in her brain fell into place.

I need to go home, she realized with a sob. She put her head down and began to cry. The sound of gunshots startled her out of her tears and she started, looking at the door.

"Stay here," the officer said, running to the door and pulling his firearm. He listened at the door and then cracked it open, leaving her alone in the room. There was silence, and she let her imagination run wild until she heard the sound of laughter and footsteps. She knew that laughter. It was Jupiter, and she knew that he had come for her.

She broke out in a cold sweat, praying that he would spare her life and leave her alone. She begged God to let her live. *If you get me out of this*, she silently cried, *I'll go home, I'll stay with Mom, I'll go home, I swear.* Tears fell down her face as she continued her silent vigil. *Even if she just hires me to work at the hotel, it's better than a life with him.*

She squeezed her eyes shut, and a picture of her mother at the Samaritan Hotel popped into her head. She hadn't thought of her mother's hotel, where she had retired, in months, but she held on to that picture with everything inside of her. Once, it had been the place where she was trapped, forced to help her mom. But now, she would give anything to be back there.

A soft knock at the door had her shaking, before a calm voice said, "Savannah, it's Officer Huber." She gave a sigh of relief as he walked in.

"We have Jupiter in custody," he said.

"Who was shot?" she whispered, trembling.

He tilted his head, and looked at her, something like sympathy in his eyes.

"No one was injured."

Savannah put her head in her hands. He finally got caught. He couldn't hurt anyone else. She took a meditative breath and looked up. The officer had more to say, she could tell.

"Is there anything else?" she asked.

He paused. "Do you feel safe here?"

"No," she answered immediately. She could feel his presence and wanted it gone. She started shivering, and the officer's face softened.

"All right," he said. "We are going to work on setting your bail, is there someone who can post bail for you?"

Savannah thought of her mom, but there was no way she could call her. Not now, not like this. She needed a better strategy.

"Not right now," she said.

Officer Huber leaned back into the chair and took a breath. "I'm going to keep you in this questioning room with one of my officers. We're holding Jupiter in our jail cell until he can be transferred to a more secure location, but he needs to stay here for at least a couple of hours."

"That's fine," she said. "Can I get the cuffs removed?"

He reached over and unlocked her hands, and she rubbed her wrists, easing the pain. A woman in uniform walked in and offered to escort her to the bathroom. At this point, her head-ache was a combination of no sleep, stress, and the coming down from all the stuff in her system, so when she looked in the mirror in the bathroom and saw her hollow eyes, pale face, and limp hair, she sighed. There was nothing she could really do except splash some water on her face, finger-comb her hair, and walk back to the interrogation room with this woman. Inside, Savannah found a blanket and a cot waiting for her. She lay down and sank into a night of bad dreams and restless breathing.

The next morning, she was escorted into the women's holding cell, where she sat and thought about her next steps. She needed to get home, but she didn't know how. The more she thought of what had happened, the more frightened and hopeless she became.

It didn't help that the food they gave her was horrible, so there was nothing but water in her system. She was afraid to ask for a cup of coffee, shuddering at the thought of the police station swill, and tried to stay as quiet and still as possible.

"That's her," she heard a voice whisper. Savannah turned and saw one of the officer's heads peek around the corner. Ashamed, she lowered her gaze and tried to blink away the tears. There was nothing left for her here. Again she felt the pang of missing home.

Around lunch, the officers moved her to the interrogation room again. This time, a smartly dressed man sat at the table, a briefcase open beside him.

"I'm Mark Brando, a defense attorney." He started rambling off a lot of information that Savannah had a hard time keeping up with. He said that her mother had hired him to represent her, and he wanted to speak with her while they were still in the station. Apparently, he had watched the tape of her confession with Julie.

Savannah was shocked that her mother knew where she was, but even more shocked that she had hired a lawyer for her. As he kept talking, her headache came back, this time with a pounding torture that settled behind her eyes. She rubbed her temples, and Brando slowed down.

"So," he took a breath and laughed at her confused expression. "My plan. I believe that the DA will want to chase Jupiter and the rest of the gang, not you. So I think that there is an opportunity for you to turn state's witness."

"What does that mean?" she asked.

"The state is building a case against him, and the fact that you confessed already looks good for *your* case. If you agree to testify against Jupiter at *his* court case, I can make a deal with the DA for you to get a lesser sentence. You will also have to give up the names of the members that you know, and testify in their trials."

Savannah shifted nervously in her seat. Her throat was dry, and she swallowed, trying to bring moisture back.

The rational part of her knew that Jupiter deserved jail time. And, if she testified against him, he could never hurt her again. Another part of her still wanted a beer and for him to hold her.

"Okay," Savannah said, finally. "I'll do it."

"Great!" Brando said. "Let's get started."

Because Savannah was a vulnerable witness, and because the case involved gang activity, Brando recommended that she remain in police custody until she had finalized a plea deal and could be admitted to the Federal Witness Protection Program.

"That's pretty serious," she said, nervously.

"We take organized crime seriously in the United States," he said. "I want you to be safe, especially if we find out that his network crossed state lines. Let's get you somewhere safe."

"How long do you think that's going to take?" she asked, thinking about her mom and her her promise to herself.

"At least a couple of months, but I can make the deal with the state for you in about a week. Before we go on, though, I need to know the facts of how you were arrested."

Savannah explained that she had tipped off the police about Jupiter, but they caught her instead of him.

"Where did you call them from?" he asked.

"My cell phone," she answered. "They took it from me when I was arrested."

Brando scribbled down more notes and kept asking her questions about what kind of information was on her phone and what she could obtain. She explained that she and Jupiter both kept copious records of their punishments on their phones, including pictures of every guest with their victims.

"He called it his insurance," she said as her stomach recoiled. She thought of the pictures and put her head in her hands. Brando paused, giving her a second to collect her thoughts.

"Do you have any pictures of Jupiter? Any videos or recordings?"

Savannah thought. "I have some pictures of the two of us, and maybe some others. I can't really remember." She was fading, and Brando could tell.

"Do you need anything?"

"A change of clothes." Her dress was too revealing for this new person she realized she wanted to be. She decided to call this person Smart Savannah.

Smart Savannah wore sweatpants and agreed with whatever the police told her to do. Smart Savannah didn't miss her psycho ex-boyfriend. Smart Savannah drank water, not beer. Smart Savannah called her mother. *Well, maybe not that last one,* she thought.

The next day, Brando brought her a change of clothes, a cup of coffee, and some news. The DA had officially offered her a deal. They wanted her to serve as state's witness, so they were going to place her in a safe house that day, but the terms of her plea deal were still being ironed out.

She was being charged with criminal assault and battery, and accessory to attempted murder. Smart Savannah nodded, but inside Savannah wanted to throw up again. Those were big, scary words. She hadn't even thought of them during the punishments. She was a criminal. Even Smart Savannah was panicking.

"What else do you need for my plea deal?" she asked.

"We'll enter your taped confession into evidence, and I want to settle as soon as possible. Until then, we need to get you somewhere safe, preferably out of town, until we can catch and charge all the members of the POTG gang."

She nodded, relieved. "What is my part in the case against Jupiter?" Her breath hitched when she said his name, which made her angry.

"The evidence against Jupiter is pretty incredible. There's so much of it, but they need you to help the jury make sense of all the information. The police took your phone and found tons of pictures and videos that place him at the crime scenes."

They were still pulling phone records but were eager to get her written agreement to testify, so she was the DA's focus as of right now. Police escorted her to an armored car, locked her inside with guards, and drove for hours into the woods to a small cabin. There, she waited.

She had a team of agents that were with her at all times, but her favorite was a burly older man named Lyle. The other men and women either stared at her like she was a zoo animal or pretended she didn't exist, but Lyle was a quiet man, who spent his days on the couch reading mystery novels or working out in the back-yard. She started joining him, pushing herself harder and harder, trying to sweat the alcohol and drug withdrawal out of her system. During the days, she wandered around the cabin, sometimes sitting for hours in one place, sometimes constantly moving. But always, thinking. Smart Savannah cooked twice a day, but at night she couldn't sleep—her mind could never shut off.

Once a week, Brando came to visit. One time, he brought paperwork for her to sign, but mostly they worked on her testimony. He grilled her relentlessly. One day, she snapped.

"Why did you do what he told you to do?" he asked.

"I don't know!" she screamed for the third time. Lyle followed her as she ran into the woods, collapsing on the ground and crying. He sat back, watching her cry, and when she had cried it all out, he followed her back.

"Why did you do what he told you to do?" Brando asked again, this time with a gentler tone.

"Because I thought we were in love," she answered. He moved onto the next question.

Soon, the DA started showing up during Brando's visits. Savannah was ready for every question, every time. The date of Jupiter's trial grew closer and closer, and her days were more restless. She was sleeping now, but there was nothing restful about it. She had this recurring nightmare where Jupiter pulled out a gun and shot the judge, and then held it to her head.

"Guilty," he would say before pulling the trigger. She always woke up screaming. Lyle started sleeping outside her door with earplugs, so she could see him when she woke up. His presence calmed her.

During the endless days of wandering the house, she had a lot of time to think about how she would get home. There was no contact with the outside world, minus what the DA allowed her, but she started to imagine what it would be like when she did see her mom. She wasn't allowed to have contact with the outside world, but she imagined their meeting almost every day.

"Mom," she always started by saying, out loud. There was always a pause, and then she couldn't think of anything else. Her words always stuck in her throat. Eventually she abandoned the attempt. She thought about calling her sister Mary. Savannah hadn't heard from her sister in years.

After intense negotiation, Brando had finalized the best deal possible for her with the DA. She pled guilty and agreed to turn state's witness against Jupiter and any other member of the POTG club who would stand trial for the crimes committed during the club's active period. In return, she would receive four years of supervised parole, spent in witness protection or a safe house until the authorities determined that she was not in imminent danger. Altogether, she knew this was the best-case scenario, especially because of how often Brando told her it was.

"You're so lucky," he said constantly. His regular presence was beginning to annoy her, but she kept it to herself. Smart Savannah knew that Brando was saving her life and was grateful for all he was doing. But, in her moments of weakness, she thought about walking out of the house, into the woods, and never coming back.

In those moments of quiet reflection, she knew that God was there, but she shoved that awareness back alongside all the experiences she had in the club. Her family had gone to church when she was a kid, but after her dad died, church fell to the back burner. Her mom had a great relationship with God, always praying for her daughters, and Savannah missed the peace that religion had brought her. After her dad died, she hadn't been interested in a God who let bad things happen. But now, in her weakest moments, she felt desperate. She needed something to remind her of the good in the world. Maybe that something was God.

But every time she sat down to pray, she was overcome with shame and guilt, so she kept ignoring the gentle, insistent voice in the back of her mind, urging her closer to Him.

One day, she was cooking and she picked up a knife wrong and pricked her finger.

"Ow," she whispered, bringing her finger up to examine her wound. All of a sudden she saw the girl whose finger they cut off. She dropped the knife, horrified, and backed up into Lyle.

He looked down at her, confusion in his eyes as she shook her head.

"I'm going to go take a nap," she said, and he nodded.

Those memories came up in her interviews, but she refused to dwell on them. She would do anything, *anything,* but focus on her past.

Soon, it would all be over, and it would be like a bad dream.

The day she was scheduled to testify in Jupiter's trial, Savannah walked into the courtroom in a brand-new blue dress, ready for anything. She wore her beauty like a weapon, hair pulled back into a braid that rested on her shoulder, makeup soft and demure, and her nails had been painted a soft pink. Every step, calculated. She hadn't seen Jupiter in months, so when he walked in, chained and wearing his orange jumpsuit, she didn't expect him to be smiling. Her heart hammered faster and faster, and she started taking deep breaths, trying to control the building panic. He walked in, nodded to the jury, smiled at the judge, and winked at her. Her stomach turned, and doubt crept in. What if the DA didn't win? What if Jupiter was set free?

CHAPTER 5

HUMILIATION

Mary was finishing her rounds when she heard her sister's name on a TV that was softly playing while she checked her patient's vitals.

"What?" she said, rousing her patient. He shifted and fell back asleep. She reached for his remote and turned the volume up on the TV, not caring if it woke him up again.

"The police have a man in custody who was arrested in connection with the violent POTG attacks, along with a Smythville local, Savannah Gresham. A representative of the police department issued the following statement earlier."

A woman in a bright pink jacket stood before the microphone.

"We have apprehended a man who we believe to be directly responsible for many, if not all, of the POTG attacks. It is with the help of Julie Schafer that we were able to capture him. The Smythville Police Department would like to extend our thanks."

Savannah? For a second, Mary thought it was a mistake. Her sister was no criminal. Surely she was working undercover. Behind the camera, someone asked to speak with Savannah, but the woman curtly shook her head.

"Miss Gresham is in our custody as well. We will keep you informed of any relevant information."

Mary sat on her patient's bed, too shocked to stand.

"Hey!" he snapped, waking up. "What are you doing?"

She apologized and left the room, making a beeline for her station.

"I'm feeling sick. I'm going home," she said, grabbing her things without apologizing to her glaring charge nurse.

Mary drove straight home and called her mother, who was working at the hotel.

"Did you hear?" she asked carefully. Since, even after all this time, her mother continued to maintain the boundary: she would not discuss her youngest daughter.

"Yes," her mother replied. "I hired a new employee today, and she's watching the hotel while I meet with a lawyer. I'll be back late."

Mary was enraged. Her mother was meeting with a lawyer? On behalf of *Savannah?* She swallowed her anger with a few breaths and paced around the house, waiting. When she didn't come home, Mary turned on the TV, which was still on her mom's favorite Christian network.

Mary's schedule made it hard to go to church and her relationship with God had turned into a chore over the years, so when she saw the Bible teacher, the first thing she felt was guilt. She settled down and listened to the sermon.

This particular teacher was discussing Luke 15, the parable of the lost sheep and coin.

"Can you imagine," the teacher asked, "that the God who created the universe would do anything to bring you back to Him? Think about how He would do the same for those around you. Are we going out of our way to love His flock? Do we view the lost as hopeless causes, or as something to be found?"

Mary turned off the TV and went to bed. But that phrase, *hopeless causes or something to be found*, echoed over and over again. Surely, the teacher couldn't mean Savannah. Could she?

Mary went into work the next morning determined not to talk about her sister. She didn't need to worry; everyone was talking about how the police had finally caught Jupiter, the leader of the POTG club. When she went to take the vitals of her patient, the latest victim, he asked her what had happened. She told him what she knew, that the police were saying that they caught the leader of the POTG club and that he had been caught in a reporter's car.

She left the whole "my sister is probably his girlfriend and she might have been the one to cut you up" part out. She had thought about it all night, and the more she thought about Savannah, the more angry she became.

She left the patient's room and saw Korban. She smiled at him, going to hug him, but he just nodded and walked away.

Mary paused. Was he ignoring her? She thought about it all day, overanalyzing every conversation, every interaction. By the end, he was returning her smiles, and she thought everything was fine. Until she overheard him talking with their charge nurse in a room while she walked by.

"They're saying Savannah Gresham is part of this. Isn't she Mary's sister?" he said quietly.

"She is," their charge nurse answered, "But Mary hasn't spoken to her in years."

"That's what she says," he responded. "But I don't know who to trust anymore."

The pit in Mary's stomach turned into a boulder. She clocked out and went home to find an empty house, as usual. She texted her mother, asking her if she was going to be home, but got no response. She checked her mom's location and saw that she was at the hospital, probably checking on Jerome.

Mary's shame deepened. She was thinking of herself when she should have been thinking of Jerome. He was finally going to get justice. Of course her mother had gone to check on him. Mary sighed and decided to heat up some leftovers. As she sat at the kitchen table and pushed food around her plate, she thought about what she wanted to do. Should she try to contact Savannah?

A knock on the door interrupted her thoughts, and she panicked for a second. Jupiter was in prison, but what about the rest of the group? Did they know that she was Savannah's sister? She had decided to ignore the knocking when her phone rang. Unknown number. She answered it, hesitantly.

"Hello?"

"Mary?" A woman's voice came through, setting her at ease. "This is Molly from the hospital."

Mary remembered. Molly was one of the victims who was a former prostitute. She and Jerome had become friends because their post-op rooms had been right next to each other. She had been admitted with trauma to her genitalia and a note stapled to her breast.

"How did you get this number?" she asked.

"You mother gave it to me. I'm working at her hotel. She sent me over with some food. Can you please let me in? I'm at your front door."

Mary was startled enough to let her in, and she grabbed the pizza from her hands. The two of them sat at the kitchen table, eating and making small talk. Molly asked her some questions about the hotel, and Mary answered them as best she could.

"How are your wounds doing?" Mary asked.

"Actually, the one on my chest still hurts a lot." Molly pulled her t-shirt back. One of the staple wounds had scarred over, but the other still looked red. There was a fresh scab on it.

"Does it itch?" Mary asked, grabbing some rubbing alcohol and ointment from the kitchen.

"Literally all the time," Molly replied, going to scratch it. Mary gently smacked her hand away, dipped a cotton swab in the rubbing alcohol, and dabbed it on the scratch. Molly flinched, so Mary paused before dabbing a little more. The kitchen was silent as she cleaned the wound, put some ointment on it, and covered it with a bandage.

"Don't scratch or pick at it," she said firmly.

"Yes ma'am." Molly saluted her, and they laughed.

Mary went to wash her hands in the kitchen sink. While she faced away from Molly, she asked, "Did you scratch it on purpose?"

Quietly, Molly answered, "Yes."

Mary grabbed a glass out of the cabinet and filled it with water, bringing it over to her.

"Do you want to talk about it?"

"Not really." Molly took a long drink and cleared her throat. "It helped me stay grounded while I healed, and then it became a habit."

Mary nodded. Sometimes pain became the thing that grounded people, but she had seen it get out of hand. A lot of her patients who had traumatic injuries used self-harm as a coping mechanism, so she was careful with her next words.

"Molly, what happened to you was wrong. Your body was hurt, but so was your mind and your soul. Does this cut hurt like the one on your soul?"

Molly nodded, tears streaming down her face.

Mary paused, wanting to treat this woman gently.

Mary pulled her chair closer and held her hands. "You didn't do anything to deserve all the pain. You deserve happiness and wholeness. Healing is a process, and you're on your journey."

Molly sat and cried for a minute longer, so Mary held one hand and put tissues in the other. When Molly had cried it all out, she gave Mary a watery smile and blew her nose.

"Next time, let's do this at my place," Molly said, and they laughed. Molly insisted on leaving the leftover pizza for Mary's mother and gave her a hug as she left. Mary felt at peace for the first time all day. She went to bed before her mom came home and left for work the next morning before her mother got up.

Over the next few weeks, things calmed down around the hospital. Her fellow nurses seemed to let her off the hook for being siblings with Savannah, and she was busy with work and her mother. They continued to have dinner once a week, and whenever she asked about Savannah, the only thing her mom could say was, "She's safe."

Mary had given up her attempts to learn any information about her absent sister when the news began dropping hints.

Reporters started mentioning an anonymous witness with personal connections to Jupiter. Mary knew it was Savannah. It made sense. She was probably in custody somewhere, waiting for the trial to start.

The trial. Savannah was going to be facing Jupiter again. A sisterly pang of sympathy hit her, and she wondered whether or not her mother was going to go to the trial.

Of course she's going. Am I?

Mary thought about the trial, her sister, and what she knew about the crimes. As one of the nurses, she was very familiar with the medical side of the crimes, but she wondered about the person on the other side. Why would someone do this? Why would her *sister* do this? She knew that she had to go, to support her mother and to get her own questions answered.

The day the trial started, Mary pulled up to the courtroom, preparing herself to see her sister. Her mom was hugging a man who looked a little older than Mary. When she walked up, her mother broke away and swiped at her eye.

"Mary, my love, this is Mark Brando. He is Savannah's lawyer."

Mark smiled and held out his hand. "Your mother's told me so much about you."

Mary shook his hand and followed him in. He held the door open and she nodded her thanks, nerves growing with every step. They settled into a bench in the courtroom and watched the selection of the jury. Savannah wasn't even there. Mark explained that she wouldn't be present until she was called as witness.

Then why are we here? Mary thought.

At the beginning of the trial, it had been leaked that the DA was bringing seventy charges of criminal assault and battery, three of rape, one of domestic abuse, and one of attempted murder. The first day, the judge sorted through the jury, which was mind-numbingly boring. Mark had been explaining the court proceedings to her, and when he explained about the dismissed evidence, Mary felt panicked. But he assured her this was normal. Almost half of the evidence that the defense tried to enter in had been dismissed, and he showed her a picture of Savannah and Jupiter that hadn't made the cut.

"Why even attempt to bring it into evidence?" she whispered as the judge dismissed another juror.

"Because they have to do their due diligence. Even if something might not stick, they have to try it."

The first day was incredibly long and drawn out, and Mary decided not to go back until Savannah was called. She exchanged phone numbers with Mark and walked with her mom back to the car.

"How do you think that went?" her mother asked, chirping her car.

Mary shrugged. "How do *you* feel?"

Her mother grinned at her. "It's going to be boring for the next couple of days, you should head back to the hospital. Your patients need you."

Mary grinned back, savoring her mother's praise as she hopped in the passenger seat. "Yes, ma'am."

Testimonies finally rolled around a week later. Savannah was scheduled to appear before the court on a Wednesday. It just so happened that Mary had Wednesdays off. She walked into the courtroom with Mark, who reached out and gave her hand a squeeze. Surprised, she looked at him.

"It's going to be okay," he said. She gave him a shaky smile, and they found their seats. The DA called Savannah to the stand, and she walked up wearing a pretty blue dress. Mary recognized the dress from a bag of clothes her mother had brought home a few weeks earlier. She felt a pang of something that felt suspiciously like jealousy, but she swallowed it down.

She saw her mother look over at her, and she subconsciously adjusted her posture, straightening her shoulders and sitting straighter.

"Please state your name for the record," the DA began.

"My name is Savannah Gresham," she said, clearly and confidently.

"What is your relationship with the defendant?"

"We were romantically involved for the last two years."

"Are you still romantically involved with him?"

Savannah paused, looking Jupiter dead in the eyes. "No."

A shiver went down Mary's spine. Jupiter shifted in his seat, losing a watt in the smug grin he seemed to have permanently affixed to his face.

It went on like this for a while. The case focused on the three counts of rape, the one attempted murder, three of the assault cases, and the domestic violence. When Savannah refused to punish one of their victims, Jupiter had smacked her across the face in a fit of violent rage.

"He apologized afterwards," Savannah said, "but I still needed stitches."

"See Evidence Document Number 45 for the medical record," the DA told the jury.

Savannah dutifully answered all of the DA's questions, and at times Mark mouthed along with her. It was clear that they had practiced this. Mary was less interested in the answers and more interested in her sister's demeanor. She seemed cool and calm, not scared of Jupiter at all. She delivered her answers in a very matter-of-fact manner. It wasn't until the end of the line of questioning that she began to squirm.

"Why do you think Jupiter did what he did?" the DA asked.

"Objection! Speculative," Jupiter's lawyer called.

"Sustained," the judge answered.

"Miss Gresham," the DA tried again, "did Jupiter ever have a conversation with you about his motivation for forming the Punishers of the Guilty club?"

"Yes," Savannah answered.

"What reasons did he give in this conversation?"

"He felt that it was his responsibility to bring justice to our town."

"When did this conversation take place?"

"It was after the third victim."

"Did you ever discuss with Jupiter his motivations after the initial conversation?"

Savannah cleared her throat and took a drink from the glass in front of her before answering.

"Yes, we had a conversation after the attack on Mr. Gorinski."

"What was his motivation then?"

Savannah swallowed. "I asked him why we attacked an innocent man. He said that he wanted to make sure that we would all do what he asked whenever he asked it, even if it was to help kill someone."

Jupiter's lawyer broke in again. "Objection! Relevance."

The DA spoke up. "It speaks to the motivation behind the attack on Jerome Gorinski as murderous in nature, not assault."

"I'll allow it," the judge said.

Mary felt for her sister. She had been trapped in a relationship where she had no real power. But then she reminded herself that Savannah had known who he was when she chose him.

Nonetheless, Mary was anxious for her sister as Jupiter's lawyer stood up.

"Here we go," murmured Mark, shifting nervously.

CHAPTER 6

A MOTHER'S STRUGGLE

"Mom!"

Lydia heard her youngest daughter call her name into the house, and she paused, remembering the first time baby Savannah had called her "Mom." Being a mother was her greatest calling, her favorite title, and an identity that had settled in like a long-awaited hug.

This time, she knew that her teenage daughter was not calling her for happy reasons. Lydia had seen her grow more and more distant over the last year, but she didn't have it in her to let her leave. Savannah had graduated a year prior, and had worked in the motel, but Lydia could tell she was unhappy. She spent hours on her phone, and every free second was spent at the gym, training until she came home with bloody knuckles and tired muscles.

Savannah walked into her bedroom, a determined look on her face. Lydia watched her daughter build up her courage. She waited for Savannah to speak first.

"We need to talk about my future," Savannah began, tapping her fingers on the side of her leg.

"Have a seat," Lydia said, pointing to her bed. The two of them sat together, and Savannah took a shaky breath.

"I would like to move out."

Lydia nodded. "All right. Where are you going to live?"

"I met a guy, and I'm going to move in with him."

Lydia tried to keep her features schooled. Who was this guy?

"Are you moving far?" she asked.

Suddenly, Savannah's face changed. She jumped up and started yelling, a fiery anger in her gaze.

"Why does it matter? Can't you just let me go?"

It was as if she had finally broken the surface of some new part of her independence. Lydia was shocked into silence, listening as her daughter continued.

"You let Mary move out, but you kept me trapped here for this whole year! Do you think I like working at the hotel? I am suffocating there! I need to leave, to see the world, to experience things!"

"And how do you expect to pay for these things?" Lydia responded, a touch too sharply.

Savannah lost some of her bravado. "With my college fund."

Lydia's heart dropped. "Honey, that money is for you to go to college."

Savannah rolled her eyes. "You know I'm not going to college. I need that money to start my new life."

Lydia was torn. One part of her wanted to fight, to fight for her daughter and her future. The other part of her knew that fighting would only make things worse.

She looked up at her daughter. There was a crazy look in her eyes that she recognized as fear, desperation, and a small ray of hope. This was the same look that her patients had before a life-changing operation.

Lydia sighed. Savannah sighed and sat down.

"Please?" she whispered. Lydia nodded and Savannah squealed, jumping up and running to her bedroom.

The next few days passed in a haze of transferred bank statements, moving trucks, and one last goodbye. Savannah gave her a hug.

"Mom, if I'm going to be doing this myself, I need you to let me do it myself."

"What does that mean?" Lydia asked.

"You have to let me go. I'm not saying that you can't text me. I'm just saying that this is it. I'm leaving."

Lydia felt a sob wrench her heart. She reached out to hug her daughter again, but decided just to kiss her cheek.

"Savannah!" she called as her daughter got in her cab. "You are always welcome to come back home!"

Savannah waved and Lydia watched the cab disappear down the street.

That was the last time she had seen her daughter until tonight.

Lydia had taken up a prayer vigil after the POTG club started terrorizing the town. She still had no idea whether Savannah was still in town, but she started every day on her face in her prayer closet, praying for the safety and protection of both her daughters. Every day, she prayed that both of them would learn to recognize the voice of the Holy Spirit and that they'd be surrounded with a hedge of protection.

Her prayers were the only thing she had. Savannah had never responded to her texts, and Mary insisted that she was fine. The older Mary got, the more she became like her. Lydia was so incredibly proud of her oldest daughter, but she didn't feel like Mary knew that.

Lydia knew that she needed to keep her home and her heart open to her girls, so she worked hard to maintain open doors. Mary had moved back home, and she knew that her second daughter was not far off. Every day, she knew it more and more.

One night, she could not sleep. Something was wrong, again. Her phone rang.

"Hello?" she said.

"Mrs. Gresham?" she heard a woman say. "I hate to be the bearer of bad news, but we have your daughter Savannah in custody."

Lydia was stunned. "Savannah Gresham?"

"Yes, ma'am."

Lydia tried to collect her thoughts. "What happened?" she asked, grabbing her purse and walking out of the door.

"She was arrested in connection with a drug deal, and she revealed that she has ties to the POTG club."

The woman at the other end delivered this life-altering information in the coolest, most matter-of-fact voice. Lydia sat frozen in the driver's seat.

"My daughter?" she whispered into the phone.

The woman at the other end was silent. Lydia cleared her throat.

"Is she okay?" she asked. "Did she ask for me?"

"No, ma'am. In fact, she asked that we not contact you, but you are her listed emergency contact."

"I'll be right there," Lydia replied, starting her engine.

The drive to the police station was one of the longest drives of her life. It was like she hit every red light in their town, and when she finally arrived at the station, there were officers positioned outside.

"What happened?" she asked, tentatively stepping out of the car.

"We caught another one of them."

The officer nearest to her smiled, but she didn't have the strength to smile back. She walked in and shook the police chief's hand. Officer Bennet had been the one to tell her of her husband's death, and Lydia was close friends with his wife.

"Where is she?" Lydia asked.

"She's in an interrogation room. We caught her boyfriend, who we think might be the man behind the whole POTG club, in our parking lot. She wants to be kept away from him."

Lydia swallowed. "Can I see her?"

"You could even talk to her if you wanted," Officer Bennet offered.

"No, I just want to see her."

He led her to a room with a large window looking into the interrogation room. Savannah sat at the table, facing away from the window. But Lydia saw her daughter. She reached out to touch the glass, and Savannah shifted in her seat, as if she felt her mother's presence. Lydia noted that she was shivering.

"She needs a jacket," Lydia whispered, pulling her hand back and leaving the room.

"Lydia," Officer Bennet called after her, as she walked down the hallway again. "What do you want us to do?"

"I'm going to hire a lawyer. He will help her much more than I can." Lydia said, the emotions of the night finally catching up to her. She wanted to be in bed. She didn't know exactly what her daughter needed, but she knew that Savannah was safe and protected, and she was content to wait on her daughter.

In the last couple years, Lydia remembered a conversation that she had with her husband when Savannah was little.

"If you offer her your help, she'll refuse it," he said. "She's independent, but she needs you to be a safe place to land when she falls."

At the time, he was talking about her climbing trees, but Lydia knew that it was true. She needed to be a safe place for her youngest daughter to land, when she stopped falling.

The next morning, she called a friend of hers whose son was a lawyer. Mark Brando was a good lawyer, and she trusted him. He was all too willing to take on the case, and met with Savannah that day.

Lydia spent the next few weeks reading Brando's constant text updates, fielding calls from Mary, running her hotel, and wondering where they had taken Savannah. She knew that she was placed in Federal Witness Protection, but she still worried for her daughter. Mary went from asking her ceaseless questions about Savannah to checking in on her, constantly. She knew that her daughter meant well, but she wanted her to take a breath and take care of herself. She worried that Mary was overextending herself. Lydia, herself, was exhausted, she could only imagine what her oldest daughter was feeling.

One day, after she had given the guests the wrong keys for the fifth time one day, Molly, her latest hire, gently put her arms around Lydia.

"I can take care of things here," she said. "Go home and take a nap."

Lydia nodded. She was exhausted and needed to sleep. She had not had a restful night since Savannah had left for the safe house.

Lydia hadn't heard from her daughter in years, but she always expected her to come back home when she ran out of money. She thought about that moment often—Savannah would show up on her doorstep, and she would welcome her in with a big hug. They would make cookies, and Savannah would work at the hotel with her again. Now, her fantasy involved her daughter winning a court case. *It's odd,* she thought, *how a crisis changes things.*

Brando explained that he was able to help Savannah turn state's witness. The first time he told her, she was confused.

"What does that mean?" Lydia asked him while they ate breakfast.

"It means that she will probably have a couple years of supervised parole, but they'll keep her in witness protection for at least two of those years." Brando paused to cut into his pancakes. "With organized crime, they want to be sure to eliminate any threats to her, and make sure that they utilize her confession as much as possible."

Savannah had still not contacted her. When Lydia brought her up, Brando reminded her that Savannah wasn't allowed to have contact with the outside world, and Lydia doubled down on her patience.

When the first day of the trial finally arrived, Lydia and Mary walked into the courthouse together. Mary had a steely determination that Lydia had always admired, but she privately thought that this particular instance masked her fear for her sister. Lydia introduced Brando to her oldest daughter, and noticed Brando grinning at Mary. She had never seen him smile that much. *Interesting,* she thought.

After the jury was selected, the DA presented her opening argument.

"Ladies and gentlemen of the jury. This case began because one man lost faith in our justice system. He took this distrust and anger and used it against many people, turning neighbor against neighbor, all in the name of a broken justice system. On one hand, he is correct. Many people he chose to attack had been convicted criminals. However, we live in the United States, where there needs to be a reasonable trust in our courts and juries and faith in our due processes."

Here the DA nodded to the jury and the judge.

"He took on the role of judge, jury, and executioner, but in that he committed violent atrocities that almost led to the death of one man and has left lingering physical and mental traumatic injuries in many others. We have a chance to prove him wrong, to right the wrongs that stink of false justice. Right now, you have a chance to hold him accountable. We will prove that his phone was at the location of every one of the crimes, we have photo evidence from his phone of most of the victims, and, most importantly, you will hear from many of his victims, naming him and his counterparts as their own attackers. His club was titled, 'Punishers of the Guilty.' I ask you, who is guilty in this courtroom? He was willing to overlook his own crimes to bring his own type of punishment on others. It is time for Jupiter to face the punishment for those crimes of which he is guilty."

Lydia was impressed, and raised her eyebrows at Mark. He smiled back at her.

The next couple of days were about Jupiter's exact crimes. Although it wasn't Savannah's turn to testify, Lydia went every single day, hoping to get a glimpse of her daughter, even in picture. Instead, she found herself reviled and revolted as expert witnesses and victims shared their thoughts and experiences. How could her daughter play a part in this? She watched Jupiter very carefully, the man who had turned her daughter into a monster. He was quiet, with a cruel smile permanently affixed to his face. One day, a picture of Savannah and him was entered into evidence. In the picture, she had a bruise on the left side of her face, but they were both smiling at the camera. Jupiter had his hand around her arm and was gripping her tightly.

Lydia's heart panged at the sight of her daughter, but Jupiter leaned back in his chair and smiled wider. At the break, Lydia went into the bathroom and splashed water on her face. Looking at herself in the mirror, she shook her finger at her reflection.

"Lydia. You are her mother. It's going to be okay."

She repeated that phrase over and over, in her prayers, when she drove, in the courtroom.

"It's going to be okay."

The day of Savannah's testimony finally came. Mary had joined her mother and Mark, who was thrilled that Mary was sitting next to him again. The three of them sat on the benches, and Mark reached over to squeeze Mary's hand reassuringly. *Interesting*, Lydia thought, again.

The DA had asked Lydia to choose a dress for her daughter, and she selected a beautiful blue one that was feminine and light. So, when Savannah walked into the courtroom escorted by her bodyguard, she couldn't help a smile breaking out over her face. This was her daughter, her real daughter. Her hair was braided and rested gently on her shoulder.

The DA got up and questioned Savannah, and she kept her cool well, answering the questions with poise and grace. When she stared Jupiter down, Lydia was so filled with pride that she almost cheered. After a long stream of questioning, the DA finished her turn.

"No further questions, your honor."

"Your witness," the judge said, as the DA sat down with a small smile.

Savannah took a drink of the glass of water on the stand and flipped her braid over her shoulder.

Jupiter's attorney pulled out a folder and took a picture out of it. "This is evidence piece number fourteen, a photo of Miss

Gresham pulled from her own phone." The photo appeared on the side TV screen facing the jury. It was a photo of Savannah standing over a victim, holding a joint.

"Miss Gresham, can you please explain what you're doing in this photo?"

Savannah shifted.

"I am posing in front of a victim of the POTG at the request of Jupiter."

"What are you holding."

Savannah sighed. "It's a joint." There was a rumble in the courtroom, and the judge glared from his seat.

"A marijuana joint?"

Savannah blinked at him. "Um, yes, is there any other kind?"

There were chuckles from the jury, and the DA shook her head at Savanah, who straightened up, cheeks blushing.

"Miss Gresham," the defendant continued, "do you recall the night this photo was taken?"

"I do."

"Was this your first marijuana joint of the night?"

"It was not."

"Had you ingested any other substances that night?"

"Yes. I had taken a shot of tequila," she said, glancing at the DA, who nodded at her.

"Would you say that during your time in the POTG club you were drinking alcohol frequently?"

"Define frequently," Savannah countered.

"At least one drink a day."

"Yes," Savannah said. "But I only started drinking and smoking after I met Jupiter."

The lawyer nodded and continued.

"During your time in the POTG club, you were having at least one alcoholic drink a day, and smoking marijuana, let's say once a week. Is that a fair estimate?"

She nodded. "Yes."

"And, when you were arrested, your blood alcohol content was 0.12 percent. That's over the legal limit to drive. Had you been drinking much that day?"

Savannah looked ashamed. "I had. By the time I spoke with Julie Schafer, though, it was lower. I had them check."

"Nonetheless, you have had a habit of drinking, occasionally to excess, correct?"

"Yes." Savannah looked defeated.

"Was there a single day when you did not have a drink in your system?"

"Not that I recall, no."

"Why should we trust your testimony as an accurate representation of what happened?"

Savannah broke her cool exterior. "Because the details are burned into my brain! I can't escape them! Ask me any question, about any victim, and I can tell you."

By this time, the energy in the courtroom was very restless. Mary looked like she wanted to throw up, and many of the jurors looked skeptical. Lydia fought the urge to stand up and yell, "Give her a chance!"

The lawyer looked amused. "Very well, Miss Gresham. Can you tell me about Grace Lorvey?"

"Grace Lorvey, aged 19. I caught her pickpocketing me at a grocery store. Two days later, on May 18, we kidnapped and blindfolded her. Jupiter put her hand on a cutting board. He traced her arm with the cleaver's knife and asked her to beg for forgiveness before cutting off her left thumb. While she screamed, he leaned forward and said, 'Compliments of the POTG.'

"Then, he told me to drive us to the ER. We dropped her off down the street, put her thumb in a bag, and kicked her out of the van."

Lydia shivered. The way she delivered these gruesome details was so matter-of-fact, but Savannah's hand was shaking as she leaned back into her chair. She had gotten every detail right, including things that only Grace had told the court, like the feel of the cleaver on her skin. Jupiter had told the court that his henchman had cut off the finger, but the cleaver was found in his apartment with only his fingerprints on it.

Jupiter's lawyer's face had fallen further and further throughout her monologue. When she finished, the DA was sitting back in her chair, looking triumphantly at the defense attorney who looked like he had swallowed a frog. The jury looked shocked. Lydia thought that Savannah had found her eyes in the crowd. She smiled reassuringly.

"Counselor?" the judge asked, as the lawyer fumbled with papers on the desk. "Any further questions?"

Jupiter looked at his lawyer, waiting for him to continue, but all the lawyer said was, "No further questions, your honor."

Savannah got down from the stand, and Jupiter made to reach out, but her bodyguard quickly stepped in, glaring at him and shaking his head. Lydia let out a small sigh of relief and looked over at Mary and Mark. They both looked slightly shell-shocked, but she felt good. Savannah had kept her cool, maintained eye contact, and had perfect recollection. Lydia wouldn't be surprised if Jupiter was found guilty on all accounts.

CHAPTER 7

JUSTICE

Life was consistently unexpected, and when Lydia came to court the next day, the judge opened up with asking the DA if she had anything to say before court proceedings began.

"Yes, your honor. We have a plea deal to enter into the record. Jupiter will plead guilty to count number four of assault and battery in exchange for information, and we will call for two years jail time."

"Very well. Jupiter, how do you plead on count number four?"

Jupiter had the audacity to wink at the DA before saying, "Guilty, your honor."

The judge banged his gavel and called on the next witness.

"What just happened?" Lydia asked Mark.

"He had been holding back the name of his right-hand man. After Savannah's testimony, they knew that he was going to be guilty of it no matter what, so they backed off. I think they'll focus on the domestic assault next."

Mark was right. They called an expert witness to the stand who established the definition of domestic abuse, and from there things took off. Lydia didn't know why she attended all the proceedings, but she did know that the hotel was in good hands with Molly. She had just hired her, but things were already going smoothly. Molly was her angel, sent from heaven, and

Lydia had already given her a raise. She noticed that Molly and Mary were spending time together, constantly hunched over her phone, giggling at something. Lydia loved that her daughter was making friends, loosening up. She had started inviting Mary to church on Sundays, and Mary had attended with her a couple of times, choosing to sit with Julie Schafer, the reporter who broke the story about Jupiter.

Every court day, Lydia and Mark walked into the courtroom together. Sometimes, Mary joined them, but for the most part, Lydia sat in the audience and prayed. The day finally came for closing statements.

Savannah had been placed back into a safe house. Mark reported that she hadn't wanted to adopt a different identity, so she elected to stay in the safehouse with her bodyguard until the cases against Jupiter and his cronies were settled. Lydia wished she was here to see the arguments.

The DA stood up, smoothing her skirt and turning on her heel to face the jury, and presented her closing remarks.

"Ladies and gentleman of the jury, I once again ask you for justice. This man, Jupiter, is a threat, a danger to our society. His twisted view of justice, of guilt and its appropriate punishment, makes him a danger to every single person he comes in contact with. We have established that he craves violence, taking pleasure in the pain of others. I ask you, can such violence ever be justified? We see that he even attacked the woman he loved, proving he has no control over his anger or his violent tendencies. To dismiss his actions, to validate his cruelty would be to do a disservice to not only his former victims but his future ones. I promise you, if he is not brought to justice, Jupiter will be back on the streets, searching for opportunities to indulge his violent desires. It is up to you to stop him."

There was silence as she sat down. The judge called for Jupiter's lawyer. Lydia had grown to hate this man through the last couple of weeks, and tuned him out, hearing bits and pieces of a disappointing, half-hearted attempt to discredit the witnesses, and call on the jury for mercy.

The judge sent the jury to deliberate. Lydia and Mark met Mary at the diner for lunch and then discussed the outcome of the trial. Lydia believed that the jury would reach a verdict soon, but Mark was less optimistic, guessing more time, at least a couple days. They were both wrong, as the jury took a solid week and a half to deliberate.

During the week, Lydia went to pray, every day. Every day, she listened and heard the voice of the Holy Spirit: *I am with you.* This one phrase carried her through and when she finally got the call from Mark, she had an overwhelming sense of peace as she drove to the courthouse. He and Mary were already there, and Lydia walked up to them, texting Molly that she would not be in that day.

They sat in their seats, smiling at Julie, the reporter, who they had seen on and off through the court proceedings. They all stood up as the judge came in and then sat as the jury was called in.

"Mr. Foreperson, have you reached a verdict?" the judge asked.

"We have," the man answered. He pulled out a paper and started reading. "We the jury find Jupiter guilty without a reasonable doubt on all counts."

There was a cheer in the courtroom and the judge banged his gavel.

"There will be order in my court," he boomed.

Jupiter's smile disappeared.

The judge continued, but all Lydia heart were the words "guilty without a reasonable doubt on all counts." She looked over to her oldest daughter, but Mark was hugging her, and she was hugging him back. Lydia smiled. When Mary saw her looking, she let go, quickly, and looked sheepishly at her mother. Lydia winked at her and kissed Mark's cheek, as he blushed and kissed her cheek back. Mary playfully smacked him, and they all held in their giggles as the judge continued.

Weeks later, at his sentencing hearing, Jupiter received twenty-five years for attempted murder, ten years for the two assault and battery cases, and two years for domestic abuse.

Lydia was ecstatic. He was guilty, guilty, guilty, and finally everyone agreed. She immediately started preparing for her daughter to come home. She couldn't be positive that Savannah would want to come home, but she secretly began to clean her room and replace the clothes in her wardrobe.

Over the next couple of years, Lydia watched from a distance as the courts found each member of the POTG guilty, and one by one they were locked up. The FBI got involved with the out-of-state members, and every day, Lydia waited for her daughter to come home. Mary started dating Mark Brando and continued to live with her mom.

Lydia wrote Savannah a letter every week and gave it to Mark. She didn't know how many of her letters Savannah actually read, but writing them helped her to feel connected to her daughter.

One day, about a year into her witness protection, one of the members of Jupiter's online forum seemed to track her down, so Savannah was moved. To where, Lydia had no idea. She lived in fear for months before realizing that was no way to live. Instead, she went to the church and spent hours in prayer, pouring out every fear and anxiety before the Lord. When she left the altar that day, she had overflowing peace.

Months later, after the last man had been sentenced, Mark told her that Savannah was finally coming home.

"When?" Lydia asked, hardly daring to believe it was true.

"I can't tell you specifics," Mark said, laughing. "Be patient."

Lydia was done being patient. She wanted to see her daughter. So she started texting Mark every day, *Is today the day?* He dutifully responded to her texts every day, *No, not yet.*

One day, she got a call from Mark.

"Hello?"

"Ask me if today is the day?" he asked her.

"Is today the day?" Lydia yelled into the phone.

"Yes! She's on a flight right now that lands in an hour."

Lydia was ecstatic. She was going to see her daughter! She jumped in the car, unable to wait any longer, and drove to the airport, ready to hug her daughter and to bring her home.

CHAPTER 8

HOME

Savannah shifted in her seat and nervously started to braid her hair. She had spent two years in witness protection, and it was still weird for her to hear her own name. She had two more years of supervised parole in her sentence, but there was no more threat to her life, so she had been given permission to go home. Anxiously, she thought about her plan. She had been making this plan for two years. She was going to go to her mom's hotel, get on her knees and apologize to her, begging her for a job.

At the trial, she had seen her mom and sister. Mary had looked at her with shame and disgust, but her mom had smiled. Savannah prayed that her mom would still smile. She had so much more to offer her. She had even worked at another hotel during witness protection so she could learn how to best help her mom. She would do anything to be home.

The flight attendant did one last sweep of the cabin, preparing for landing as Savannah practiced her speech under her breath.

"Mom, I am sorry for leaving you. I know you may never forgive and accept me as your daughter, but would you consider hiring me? I promise I'll work really hard and will offer a lot to the business."

She repeated her speech over and over again as the turbulence rocked the plane back and forth. Her seatmate grabbed the seat, praying in a language she didn't understand. When the plane evened out, she smiled at him, and he gave her a shaky smile back. When she landed, she texted Brando. He was going to pick her up and take her to the hotel, and then…well, she would see.

She grabbed her backpack and walked off the plane, rolling her neck and savoring the stretch in her legs. She walked to the luggage claim and looked for Brando. He was supposed to meet her there. To her surprise, she saw a woman with grey hair running toward her. Savannah kept her head down. Surely this woman was running to someone else.

"Savannah!" she heard the woman yell, and she was frozen in shock. Her mother was running up to her. Savannah barely had time to register this thought before she was hugging her, crying into her neck. Savannah didn't know what to do, so she hugged her back, crying harder. For a moment, it was just the two of them, hugging in an airport. Savannah didn't see Mark Brando smiling off to the side, or the strangers who passed them smiling. It was just the two of them. Savannah finally caught her breath and started her speech.

"Mom, I'm so sorry for leaving you…" she continued through tears that didn't stop rolling. Wordlessly, Lydia grabbed her around the neck again, wrapping her in the kind of hug that only a mother can give. Savannah started crying again, and they just stood there again.

Savannah was the first to break the hug, reaching into her pocket to grab a napkin to blow her nose. Lydia turned to Mark.

"Take Savannah to the diner. We are going to have the biggest celebration dinner together. Invite everyone you can, it's on me. I'll meet you there."

Savannah held herself together as her mother gave her one last hug and went to her own car, and Mark brought Savannah to the nearest bathroom. He handed her a change of clothes and smiled when she emerged, fresh-faced and ready.

They set off to the diner, Savannah hardly believing what had happened.

***

Mary had worked a long shift. She wanted to go home and soak in the bathtub, but she had agreed to work the night shift at the hotel. Her mother said she had plans tonight and winked at her. Mary thought that she was going to surprise her and take her to dinner, so she wasn't surprised when Molly was waiting for her with the car keys.

Molly linked their arms and dragged Mary to the car, the two of them laughing the whole time. When they turned on Main Street, Mary saw crowds of people walking toward the diner, music and laughter pouring out of the restaurant.

"What's going on?" she asked, confused.

Molly grinned. "Your sister is home!"

Mary's heart sank. This whole party was for *Savannah?*

Molly found a parking spot and got out. "You coming?" she asked when Mary didn't move.

"In a second," Mary answered. She sat in the car, practicing her deep breaths. It had been two years since Jupiter's sentencing, and she secretly hoped to never see her sister again. It was bad enough that Savannah's name was blasted all over national news, but for her to come *home?* And for her mother to throw a party with the whole town, *celebrating* her?

She had been part of the club that terrorized the town, and they were forgiving her. Mary couldn't stand it. She decided that she would stay in the car, because if she had to look her sister or, heaven forbid, her mother in the eyes, she would lose it.

***

Lydia and Savannah sat at a booth while everyone else pressed in. A local band had set up outside, and the waitresses at the diner were passing out burgers and fries as fast as the kitchen could cook them. Their favorite waitress, Elizabeth, came by and kissed Savannah on the cheek.

"Missed ya, kid," she said, giving her a wink. Savannah looked like she was going to cry. A couple of people looked angry, or wary of her, but Lydia quickly spoke up.

"Isn't it great to have her home? I can't believe how much she's changed and grown," she said.

Everyone smiled and chatted politely, but Lydia was waiting for Mary. She wanted her family to be together. Molly walked in, and Lydia was surprised to see her alone. She caught her eye, and Molly pointed to the parking lot.

Lydia smiled at Savannah and got out of the booth. She needed to have a conversation with Mary.

She walked up to the car and knocked on the window. Mary rolled it down, displeasure clear on her face.

"Why don't you come in, sweetheart?"

"No, thanks," Mary said, staring blankly through the front windshield.

Lydia sighed. "Sweetheart, what's wrong?"

Mary slammed her palm into the dashboard.

"What's *wrong*? I have worked for you for years. I never embarrassed you. I've supported you, loved you, even followed in your footsteps. You've never thrown me a party or told people you're proud of me. But when your criminal daughter—who literally ruined the lives of countless people—shows up, you throw her a party at our restaurant? With the whole town? What do I have to do to get your attention?"

Lydia went to hug her daughter through the window, but Mary drew back. Lydia sighed again.

"Honey, you are my eldest daughter, my pride and joy. Everything that I have is yours. The hotel, the house, all of it is yours. And I am so proud of you. Every time I see you, I see a beautiful, wonderful woman who astounds me."

Lydia watched as Mary's mouth twitched.

"At the same time, your sister was gone. I didn't know if she would ever come home, and at one point, I thought she was dead. But she's home now! We've got to celebrate because she's home. Will you come and eat with us?"

Mary stared at her hands for a while.

Finally, she turned the car off and got out. Together, Mary and Lydia walked into the diner. She sat next to her sister, and Lydia sat across from them. Elizabeth brought milkshakes, and Mary smiled her thanks.

Wordlessly, Savannah held up her glass. Mary looked at it, and then at her mother, who held hers up as well. She sighed, smiled, and clinked her milkshake against her sister's and mother's.

They all drank, and Mary savored the taste. It tasted like home.

EPILOGUE

In finishing up our deep dive into the Prodigal Son or Chasing Father parable, it's my deep desire that you find yourself more settled in your identity as God's beloved child. I also want to finish our journey with a brief look at Jesus' additional parables He gives just before He gave this incredible story.

Let's consider the two parables that lead into this powerful story about family, noting that all three of these parables share the common theme of lost and found. The theme of lost and found is a common human experience, regardless of the time in history and the location for the experience. I've had plenty of lost-and-found adventures, from lost headphones on an airplane, losing my driver's license, misplacing a credit card, forgetting my phone, and plenty more disturbing experiences. I can be very absent-minded!

In the first parable that Jesus gives immediately on the heels of the grumbling scribes and Pharisees, He describes how a shepherd has one hundred sheep and loses one of them. Once the shepherd realizes that he's lost a sheep, he leaves the ninety-nine to search until he finds the one that is lost. Once he finds this sheep, he puts it on his shoulders, returns home, and celebrates with his friends. He has recovered his lost sheep! In Luke 15:6 (NASB), the shepherd says, "Rejoice with me, for I have found my sheep which was lost!"

In the second parable, Jesus describes a woman who has ten coins (a complete set) and loses one of her coins. The woman lights a lamp, sweeps her house, and searches carefully until she finds her lost coin. When she finds her coin, she calls together her neighbors and friends to celebrate with her. Her celebration words are similar to those of the shepherd, "Rejoice with me, for I have found the coin which I had lost" (Luke 15:9 NASB).

Finally, in Jesus' third parable about lost and found, He drives home His point about kids being reconciled to their Father. Indeed, the father tells his servants and his oldest son the same thing in Luke 15:24 and 32, only changing the word *son* for the word *brother* to be mindful to whom the father was speaking—servants and brother.

> *"For this son of mine was dead and has come to life again; he was lost and has been found." And they began to celebrate* (Luke 15:24 NASB).

> *But we had to celebrate and rejoice, for this brother of yours was dead and has begun to live, and was lost and has been found* (Luke 15:32 NASB).

As we think about how this idea of lost and found can be applied in our lives, we must consider the gravity of the heart and intent of our Heavenly Father. When we think about and reflect on the people around us and their various conditions and existences, let's think about the possibility that people around us might be lost or disconnected from knowing the intense love and affection of their Heavenly Father for them as His son or daughter. Some people work hard to be deserving of genuine love. Some people think they're too far gone to be a son or daughter of God. Both conditions are lost because of the fundamental disconnect from the Father with each perspective.

At the same time, let's appreciate God's intense celebration that happens when the lost is found. If a shepherd is ecstatic to find his lost sheep and a woman is overjoyed to recover a lost coin, how much more is our Heavenly Father over the moon to welcome a lost son or daughter back into the family, integrated because of God's love rather than isolated because of poor decisions and righteous piety!

Let us choose to live found in our Father's immeasurable love for us, and let's be His agents of reconciliation, reflecting His love for each human as His son and daughter!

ENDNOTES

1 "Kezazah," Encyclopedia.com, 2024, https://www.encyclopedia .com/religion/encyclopedias-almanacs-transcripts-and-maps/ kezazah.

2 "1159. Dapanaó," BibleHub.com, 2024, https://biblehub .com/greek/1159.htm.

3 "Murphy's Law," Merriam-Webster.com, 2024, https:// www.merriam-webster.com/dictionary/Murphy%27s%20 Law.

4 "2853. Kollaó," BibleHub.com, 2024, https://biblehub.com/ greek/2853.htm

5 "3407. Misthios," BibleHub.com, 2024, https://biblehub .com/greek/3407.htm.

6 BetterHelp Editorial Team, "Birth Order Theory: Why it Matters," BetterHelp.com, June 18, 2024, https://www .betterhelp.com/advice/family/birth-order-theory-insights -into-your-personality/.

7 "Pais," BlueLetterBible.org, 2024, https://www.blueletterbible .org/lexicon/g3816/kjv/tr/0-1/.

8 "4697. Splagchnizomai," BibleHub.com, 2024, https://bible-hub.com/greek/4697.htm.

9 "Strong's #5143: Trecho," BibleTools.org, 2024, https:// www.bibletools.org/index.cfm/fuseaction/Lexicon.show/ID/ G5143/trecho.htm.

ADDITIONAL RESOURCES

Bailey, Kenneth E. *The Cross and the Prodigal.*
Bailey, Kenneth E. *Finding the Lost: Cultural Keys to Luke 15.*
Nouwen, Henri, *The Return of the Prodigal Son.*

ACKNOWLEDGMENTS

Mom and Dad: thank you for all your love. For all my Ministry Mafia girls: thank you for teaching me what it means to have sisters. For the Hupps: thank you for showing me the strength of family. For the Pauls: thank you for "adopting" me. For Tim: thank you for all the legal jargon. For Jesus: I love you.

ABOUT THE AUTHOR

Sarah Bowling

Sarah Bowling is on a mission to connect every one with the heart of God while loving those who are overlooked, excluded, and ignored. Led by Holy Spirit and anchored in the Word, Sarah seeks to inspire all to know the unconditional and transformational love of God in our daily lives. She is a discerning Bible teacher, an international speaker, and a global humanitarian.

As part of *Marilyn & Sarah Ministries*, Sarah co-hosts a daily television program, *Today with Marilyn & Sarah*, reaching a potential daily audience of 2.2 billion households worldwide. Sarah has been a keynote speaker at events all over the world and has also authored numerous books including *In Step with the Spirit, Hey God, Can We Talk?*, and *Your Friendship with Holy Spirit*.

Sarah is the founder of *Saving Moses*, a global humanitarian organization saving babies (5 and under) every day by meeting the most urgent and intense survival needs where help is least available. Saving Moses funds and establishes revolutionary programs in nations of the world that record the highest infant mortality rate and where babies of sex workers are most susceptible to exploitation. Visit the website at savingmoses.org.

In 2019, Sarah launched her teaching ministry, *Sarah Bowling – Living Genuine Love*. Through her books, blogs, podcasts, videos, and live teaching events, Sarah is committed to sharing life-giving revelation that will transform lives on a daily basis. To learn more, visit sarahbowling.org.

Sarah and her husband, Reece, have three children and are Lead Pastors of Encounter Church in Denver, Colorado. She holds a Bachelor of Arts degree from Oral Roberts University and a Master of Arts degree from the University of Missouri.

Isabell Bowling

Growing up under the teachings of her grandmother and mom, **Isabell** developed a passion for the Word and for loving people well. She gave her heart to the Lord at the tender age of six, but faced mental health issues and church hurt, which caused her to doubt her faith. Through this time, God never gave up on her; and in His infinite mercy and grace He brought her back into His loving embrace.

During her college years, Isabell led mission trips and was a student ministry leader. In 2023, she graduated with a degree in Historical and Philosophical Theology and Modern Hebrew from Oral Roberts University. Upon graduation she earned the honor of Outstanding Theology Student of the Year.

Since her graduation, Isabell has become an integral member of the *Marilyn & Sarah Ministry* team. She is multi-talented in writing, teaching, and ministry operations. In 2024, Sarah and Isabell released their first book together entitled *Road to Wholeness.*

During her free time Isabell enjoys leading a C.S. Lewis book club at her church, spending time with her friends, reading, dancing, crocheting, traveling, cooking, and watching movies. She is also an avid fan of tea, coffee, and Formula One racing.

Check out
our **Destiny Image**
bestsellers page at
<u>destinyimage.com/bestsellers</u>

for cutting-edge,
prophetic messages
that will supernaturally
empower you and the
body of Christ.